# TOP**10**
# MONTREAL
## AND QUEBEC CITY

# Top 10 Montreal and Quebec City Highlights

# The Top 10 of Everything

# CONTENTS

## Montreal and Quebec City Area by Area

## Streetsmart

Within each Top 10 list in this book, no hierarchy of quality or popularity is implied. All 10 are, in the editor's opinion, of roughly equal merit.

Throughout this book, floors are referred to in accordance with American usage; i.e., the "first floor" is at ground level.

***Title page, front cover and spine*** *Aerial view of the cityscape from Mount Royal Park, Montreal* ***Back cover, clockwise from top left*** *Vieux Quebec; Lac-Superieur; Ski Resort at Mont-Tremblant; Skyline of Montreal; Saint Joseph Oratory*

# Welcome to
# Montreal and Quebec City

Montreal is often called the cultural capital of Canada. Spend a few days here and it soon becomes evident why, from its charming cobblestone streets to innovative museums. Quebec City dates back to the early 17th century and is similarly rich in art and history. With Eyewitness Top 10 Montreal & Quebec City, it's yours to explore.

Montreal's Francophone roots have seeped into all aspects of life, from French-inspired cuisine to the creative theater scene. But Montreal is equally influenced by its North American heritage: in one day, you can gaze up at mirrored skyscrapers, clip-clop through **Vieux-Montréal** on a horse carriage, sip espresso at a buzzy café, and then top off the night at a rooftop club. But you haven't truly experienced Quebec until you've visited Quebec City, which is North America's oldest surviving walled city. Walk the ancient turrets of Vieux-Québec, snap photos of the **Château Frontenac**, catch a show by the homegrown **Cirque du Soleil**, and sample fresh produce at **Île d'Orleans**, known as the "Garden of Quebec."

Both cities explode with year-round festivals, from **Just For Laughs** to the **Quebec Winter Carnival**. Local museums rival the festivals, including Montreal's **Musée des Beaux-Arts** and Quebec City's **Musée de la Civilisation de Québec**.

Whether you're coming for a weekend or a week, our Top 10 guide is designed to bring together the best of everything these two cities have to offer. The guide gives you insider tips throughout, from free events and activities to the lowdown on hotels, plus easy-to-follow itineraries that tie together a slew of sights in a short space of time. Add inspiring photography and detailed maps, and you've got the essential pocket-sized travel companion. **Enjoy the book, and enjoy Montreal and Quebec City.**

Clockwise from top: **Stade Olympique, Montreal; Oratoire St-Joseph, Montreal; Marché Bonsecours, Montreal; Parc National du Mont-Tremblant; James McGill; Vieux-Port, Montreal; Ice-skaters, Quebec**

# Exploring Montreal and Quebec City

Montreal and Quebec City abound in cultural riches, from art-packed museums, historic cathedrals, and theater to festivals, parks and waterfronts. Whether here for a weekend or a week, these two- and four-day itineraries will maximize your time.

**Montreal's botanical gardens** are an oasis in the heart of the city.

## Two Days in Montreal

### Day ❶
**MORNING**

Explore at your own pace the fascinating **Musée Pointe-à-Callière** (see pp22–3), which brings the history of Montreal to life. Afterwards, saunter along Montreal's **Vieux-Port** (see pp60–67) and breezy waterfront, taking in views of the St Lawrence River along the way.

**AFTERNOON**

Stroll the cobblestone streets of Vieux-Montréal to the **Basilique Notre-Dame** (see pp16–17), a Gothic Revival masterpiece that is now the symbol of the city. Time your visit with one of the choral concerts that take place in the early evening.

### Day ❷
**MORNING**

Peruse the **Musée des Beaux-Arts de Montréal** (see pp24–5), the oldest museum in the country, which traces the artistic timeline of Canada, from antiquities to contemporary works.

**AFTERNOON**

Head to the **Parc Olympique** (see pp18–21) and explore the complex, and then visit the fragrant **Jardin Botanique** (see pp20–21). Afterwards, tour Montreal's geographic gem: the forested slopes of **Parc du Mont-Royal** (see pp12–15). Walk a mountain trail leading to scenic lookouts, and watch the sun set over the skyline, with the river glinting in the distance.

# Four Days in Montreal and Quebec City

## Day ❶

**MORNING**

Start the morning in the heart of Vieux-Montréal: enjoy an espresso at a café, and then walk the narrow, historic streets to the **Basilique Notre-Dame** *(see pp16–17)*.

**AFTERNOON**

Head down to the waterfront along the banks of the St Lawrence River, to the **Musée Pointe-à-Callière** *(see pp22–3)*, where you can learn about Montreal's history.

## Day ❷

**MORNING**

Kick off the day at the **Musée des Beaux-Arts de Montréal** *(see pp24–5)*, Montreal's most celebrated museum. Then roam the leafy pathways of **Parc du Mont-Royal** *(see pp12–15)*.

**AFTERNOON**

Take an afternoon getaway to **Les Laurentides** *(see pp36–7)*: visit Val-David, a lively town with art galleries, restaurants, and mountain views.

## Day ❸

**MORNING**

Head to Quebec City and start your explorations at the **Musée de la Civilisation de Québec** *(see pp30–31)*, which covers centuries of history.

**AFTERNOON**

Stroll the beautifully preserved alleyways of Vieux-Québec, and then

**The Musée de la Civilisation de Québec** explores the region's history.

visit the elegant **Basilique Sainte-Anne-de-Beaupré** *(see pp32–3)*, one of the oldest pilgrimage sites in North America.

## Day ❹

**MORNING**

Explore the vast **La Citadelle** *(see pp28–9)*, a military fortification that sprawls over 37 acres (15 ha). Visit for the Changing of the Guard (10am daily Jun–Sep). Bring a picnic lunch to enjoy on the verdant grounds.

**AFTERNOON**

Head to the charming **Île d'Orleans** *(see pp34–5)*, stopping to view the thundering Montmorency Falls along the way. Walk or cycle around the island, visiting vineyards, art galleries, and artisan workshops to get a glimpse into historic Quebec.

Key

━━ Two-day itinerary

━━ Four-day itinerary

# Top 10 Montreal and Quebec City Highlights

Changing of the Guard at La Citadelle, Quebec City, with Château Frontenac in the background

# TOP 10 Montreal and Quebec City Highlights

These two cities captivate with their history, culture, and festivity. Both major players in the foundation of Canada, their portside locations have kept them at the heart of commerce, resulting in a charming blend of heritage architecture and modern venues.

### 1 Parc du Mont-Royal
Looming over Montreal's bustling activity, this park is the most visited attraction in the city *(see pp12–15)*.

### 2 Basilique Notre-Dame
North America's largest church when built in 1829 is still the Gothic Revival gem of Vieux-Montréal *(see pp16–17)*.

Map of the region including: St-Michel-des-Saints, St-Ignace-du-Lac, St-Tite, Parc National du Mont-Tremblant, QUÉBEC, St-Donat, Trois-Rivières, Nicolet, Lac St-Pierre, Les Laurentides, Laurentides, Val-David, St-Félix-de-Valois, Pierreville, Ste-Adèle, Mont-Rolland, Lavaltrie, Tracy, St-Germain-de-Grantham, Rivière du Diable, Lachute, Terrebonne, Parc Olympique, St-Hyacinth, Hawkesbury, Ottawa, Laval, Châteauguay, Bromont, St-Lawrence, see Central Montreal inset

0 km  50
0 miles  50

### 4 Musée Pointe-à-Callière
The true birthplace of Montreal unites the city's history and modern technology *(see pp22–3)*.

### 3 Parc Olympique
Parc Olympique's many attractions include botanical gardens, a planetarium, and sports facilities *(see pp18–21)*.

Central Montreal

1. Parc du Mont-Royal
5. Museé des Beaux-Arts de Montréal
2. Basilique Notre-Dame
4. Musée Pointe-à-Callière

QUARTIER LATIN
CHINATOWN
DOWNTOWN
VIEUX-MONTRÉAL
VIEUX-PORT

0 meters 1000
0 yards 1000

8. Basilique Sainte-Anne-de-Beaupré
9. Île d'Orléans
6. Quebec City
7.

St-Raymond
ortneuf
Donnacona
St-Agapit
Ste-Marie
East Broughton
Daveluyville
Plessisville
Warwick
Richmond
herbrooke

### 5 Musée des Beaux-Arts de Montréal

The largest in Québec, this museum has works dating from antiquity to contemporary masters *(see pp24–5)*.

### 6 La Citadelle, Quebec City

Three centuries of military presence continue in this working army base, home to Canada's first observatory *(see pp28–9)*.

### 7 Musée de la Civilisation de Québec

Exhibits here include artifacts from the First Nations, Chinese *objets d'art*, and items from everyday life in Quebec *(see pp30–31)*.

### 8 Basilique Sainte-Anne-de-Beaupré

Featuring 240 stained-glass windows and a gleaming mosaic, this granite basilica was built in 1923–63 *(see pp32–3)*.

### 9 Île d'Orleans

This island of farm communities preserves the traditions of the original settlers *(see pp34–5)*.

### 10 Les Laurentides

Visit the mountain range that has long been the favorite year-round playground for weekenders and vacationers with its pristine lakes, hiking trails, and ski slopes *(see pp36–7)*.

# TOP 10 ⭐ Parc du Mont-Royal

The geographic highlight of Montreal is Mont-Royal's steep slopes. Named by Jacques Cartier in 1535, the protected district of Parc du Mont-Royal covers a large expanse of forested mountain, providing abundant green spaces, shrubs, and flowers, as well as habitats for hundreds of species of birds and other wildlife. Designed in 1876 by Frederick Law Olmsted, Mont-Royal still inspires locals as an arboreal delight in the center of their metropolis – activity options include skating, cycling, paddle-boating, tobogganing, and snowshoeing. To the northwest is the Oratoire St-Joseph.

### Oratoire St-Joseph ①
The dome atop this shrine is an overwhelming sight to the west of the park **(right)**. Pilgrims flock to the oratory, inspired by tales of miracle cures *(see pp14–15)*.

### ② Lookouts
Belvedere Kondiaronk **(below)** is the lookout of the Chalet du Mont-Royal. The Camillien-Houde lookout faces east over the river. Locals often refer to it as "Lovers' Lookout."

### ③ Trail Systems
The park has a network of forested corridors, popular with cyclists and runners in summer and cross-country skiers in winter.

### ⑤ La Croix
Standing 100 ft (31 m) high, the original steel cross **(right)** was erected by Paul de Chomedey, Sieur de Maisonneuve, in 1643.

### ④ Cemeteries
Cimetière Notre-Dame-des-Neiges (Catholic) and Cimetière Mont-Royal (non-Catholic) are the two main resting places of the city. Far from sombre, they are adorned with lovely statues, sculptures, and luxuriant plantings.

**Map of Parc du Mont-Royal**

### FREDERICK LAW OLMSTED

A champion of the City Beautiful movement of landscape architects, Frederick Law Olmsted was born in Hartford, Connecticut in 1822. Best known for his visionary designs of Central Park in New York City, Olmsted's aim was to reject the formal plantations that had previously been in vogue and to complement the natural landscape with his pastoral designs and with designated areas for recreation.

### 6 Police Stables

Visits to the Police Cavalry Stables are possible, and it is common to see officers on horseback cantering through the park.

### 7 Maison Smith

Built for Boston merchant Hosea B. Smith in 1858, Maison Smith is home to Les Amis de la Montagne exhibitions, and is an entry point to the park.

### 8 Les Amis de la Montagne

This is the base of a citizen group focusing on the preservation of and education about both the historic and natural legacy of the park.

### 9 Lac aux Castors

The heart of Parc du Mont-Royal is Lac aux Castors. People gather during fair weather to paddle boats or to ice-skate in winter **(above)**.

### 10 Tam-Tam Festival

Sundays in the park during the summer belong to the exuberant Tam-Tam Festival. For decades, drummers, musicians, dancers, and artisans have spontaneously gathered around the Monument Sir George-Étienne Cartier where they party until dusk.

### NEED TO KNOW

**MAP C2** ▪ (514) 843 8240 ▪ www.lemontroyal.qc.ca

*Oratoire St-Joseph:*
3800 Chemin Queen-Mary; (514) 733 8211; Mass: 7am, 8:30am, 10am, 11:30am, 4:30pm, & 7:30pm Mon–Sat, 7am, 8am, 9:30am, 11am, 12:30pm, 4:30pm, & 7:30pm Sun; www.saint-joseph.org

▪ If visiting Montreal in winter, you can still enjoy a version of the Tam-Tam Festival, as well as a drink, at the nearby El Zaz Bar *(see p82).*

▪ Parking fees are high in Parc du Mont-Royal. Park inside the grounds of one of the cemeteries and walk to the lookout.

# Features of Oratoire St-Joseph

### 1 Saint Brother André

Alfred Bessette, born in 1845, joined the Congregation of the Holy Cross in 1870. Here, as a humble cleric, he assumed the name of Brother André and began working extraordinary curative powers on the sick. He attributed his skills to St Joseph and petitioned for donations to build the Oratoire. He was canonized by Pope Benedict XVI in 2010.

### 2 Neo-Classical Architecture

Inspired by the temples of Corinth, architects Dalbé Viau and Alphonse Venne designed the exterior of St Joseph's, but the completion was a collaboration of Lucien Parent, monk Dom Paul Bellot, and architect Gérard Notebaert.

### 3 Saint Brother André's Tomb

Brother André died on January 6, 1937, at the age of 91. While his remains are buried in the church, his heart was removed and placed in a reliquary, and is still a popular draw for pilgrims. A beautiful fresco, created by Henri Charlier, decorates his tomb wall.

**Pilgrims ascending the 99 Steps**

### 4 99 Steps

There are 283 concrete steps leading from the street up to the crypt church, with 99 wooden steps in between. Dedicated pilgrims can be often seen struggling up the wooden steps on their knees.

### 5 Musée de l'Oratoire

An extensive religious art collection heads the permanent features on display in the Oratory Museum. The museum is also known for its large and unusual collection of nativity displays.

### 6 Crypt Church

Created in 1917 at the base of the basilica, the concrete structure of the crypt church is built into the mountainside and forms part of the Oratory's foundations. It has a main altar of Carrara marble and a 1,000-seat capacity. Don't miss the stunning stained-glass windows.

### 7 John XXIII Pavilion

A convenient overnight hostel adjacent to the parking area contains a souvenir shop and cafeteria. A resident organization also helps arrange personalized religious journeys for the faithful.

**Saint Brother Andre's Tomb**

## THE HISTORY OF THE ORATOIRE ST-JOSEPH

The saga of Montreal's mammoth Oratoire St-Joseph began with the construction of a tiny chapel in 1904 by Brother André and friends. The final structural elements only came together in 1967 – 30 years after Brother André's death. More than 500 ft (150 m) above street level, it is a staggering 195 ft (60 m) from the floor to the peak of the dome – one of the largest in the world. Reminiscent of Italian Renaissance architecture, the basilica features Corinthian columns, stained-glass master-pieces, and a huge carillon (56 bells). More than two million

**Oratoire St-Joseph facade**

visitors pack the monument each year, with crutches and wheelchairs left behind as evidence of the cures taking place here. Brother André's followers had long been asking for his canonization. In accordance with the Catholic church, two posthumous miracles are needed to earn sainthood. The first, the cure of a cancer victim in 1958, led to his beatification in 1982. The second was in 1999, when a boy emerged from a coma after an accident. It made Brother André the 11th Canadian, and first Quebec-born, saint.

**Canes hanging in the Votive Chapel**

### 8 Votive Chapel

Canes, crutches, and other medical aids left behind by cured pilgrims line the walls in this small but inspirational chapel. Visitors can light a devotional candle, then walk past a statue of St Joseph to the room of Saint Brother André's tomb.

### 9 Altar and Stations of the Cross

The magnificent altar, crucifix, and wooden statues of the 12 Apostles are creations of the French artist Henri Charlier. Roger Villiers sculpted the Way of the Cross between 1957 and 1959, and the stunning interior mosaic was added to the altar in 1960.

### 10 Les Petits Chanteurs du Mont-Royal

Begun in 1956 by the then head of the church Father Brault, the oratory's choir is made up of 210 boys aged between 8 and 17. Their silky vocals embellish more than 70 religious festivities each year, at the oratory, around the country, and abroad. Their repertoire ranges from Georgian chant to modern choral works. The boys are schooled here when they are not performing.

# Basilique Notre-Dame

**TOP 10** ★

The most magnificent landmark of Vieux-Montréal is this huge Gothic Revival undertaking designed by Irish architect James O'Donnell and built between 1824 and 1829. This thriving Catholic church has a stunning medieval-style interior that features walnut wood carvings, exquisite stained-glass windows, 24-carat gold stars in a vaulted blue ceiling, plus one of the largest Casavant organs in North America. Don't miss the fine art paintings in the nave and the impressive Chapelle du Sacré-Coeur hidden behind the altar.

### 1 Gothic Revival Architecture
Rectangular in shape, contrary to the norms of the day, Notre-Dame features arcades with cross-ribbed vaulting.

### 2 Le Gros Bourdon
It is possible to hear the amazing chimes of Le Gros Bourdon, the largest bell in North America, 18 miles (30 km) outside Montreal.

### 3 The Altar
In 1880 local artists Henri Bouriché and Victor Bourgeau created complementary wood sculptures backed by azure for this amazing altarpiece **(right)**.

### 4 Chapelle du Sacré-Coeur
Opened in 1891, this delightful gem **(left)** is concealed behind the main altar. Countless marriage ceremonies take place here, inspiring the moniker, "The Wedding Chapel."

**NEED TO KNOW**

**MAP K3** ■ 110 Rue Notre-Dame Ouest, Place d'Armes ■ (514) 842 2925 ■ www. basiliquenotredame.ca

**Open** 8am–4:30pm Mon–Fri, 8am–4pm Sat, 12:30–4pm Sun
Adm $6

■ **Maison Christian Faure** (355 Place Royale) serves delicate and delicious pastries as well as sweets and sandwiches.

■ Breathtaking sound and light *(son et lumière)* shows, called AURA, are held daily.

**JAMES O'DONNELL**

Irish architect James O'Donnell was contracted to draw plans and oversee the construction of Basilique Notre-Dame in 1823. A Protestant by birth, O'Donnell's pride in the basilica caused him to convert to Catholicism, allowing him burial inside "his" church. Synthesizing many divergent design elements from contributing architects, he introduced the Gothic Revival style into Canadian architecture.

### 7 Stained-Glass Windows

In 1929 Olivier Maurault, a priest and author, conceived the present-day windows **(above)**, which depict early religious events and scenes from the lives of the people of Vieux-Montréal.

**Plan of Basilique Notre-Dame**

### 8 Daudelin Sculpture

The sculptor Charles Daudelin's bronze *reredos* **(above)**, which hangs behind the Chapelle du Sacré-Coeur, is among his most dramatic works.

### 5 The Pulpit

Architect Victor Bourgeau's first known work is the 1844 spiral staircase pulpit, resembling tiers of a wedding cake. Set in the middle of the church, it allows sermons to be heard without amplification.

### 9 Famous Weddings

Many famous couples have tied the knot in Notre-Dame, but the best-known celebrity wedding is that of singer Céline Dion in 1994 *(see p43)*.

### 6 Séminaire St-Sulpice

Built in 1685 by the Sulpician order, this stone structure standing beside the basilica is the second oldest building in Montreal *(see p61)*.

### Casavant Organ 10

Blacksmith Joseph Casavant was the first significant builder of pipe organs in Canada. He built the Notre-Dame organ **(right)** for the basilica in 1891.

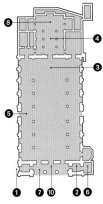

# TOP10 ⭐ Parc Olympique

One of Montreal's most remarkable attractions, Parc Olympique is also one of its most controversial. Built for the 1976 Olympic Games, it remained unfinished until the 1980s, and the retractable roof over the stadium has never fully worked. Nevertheless, visitors can easily spend a full day or two entertained by the varied exhibitions, sights, and activities within this immense quadrilateral. Ride the funicular to the top of the Tour Montréal for the most enthralling view of the region.

### Stade Olympique ①

Designed by the French architect Roger Taillibert and constructed by local engineers for the 1976 Olympics, the stadium **(right)** seats 60,000 people, has a cable-suspended roof and is covered in a membrane of space-age Kevlar material. Today it is used to stage events such as rock concerts.

### ② Centre Sportif

This sports complex houses five swimming pools with continuously recirculating water. Other facilities include a fitness suite, yoga studios, a center for scuba diving, and a café.

### ③ Aréna Maurice-Richard

Named after the Montreal Canadiens hockey legend Maurice "Rocket" Richard **(right)**, the indoor rink continues to promote the sport. The museum "Univers Maurice-Richard" features the scoring ace's memorabilia.

### ④ Planétarium Rio Tinto Alcan

Opened in 2013, this fascinating museum **(right)** has state-of-the-art technology explaining everything from the building blocks of life on earth to the many wonders of the universe (see p51).

### ⑤ Tour Montréal

For great views ride the extraordinary funicular in the Tour Montréal. An observatory sits atop the world's highest leaning tower, almost 541 ft (165 m) from ground to summit.

### ⑥ Marché Maisonneuve

More than just a taste of fresh market fare, the Marché Maisonneuve attracts clientele from all over the province, and is the perfect spot for people-watching.

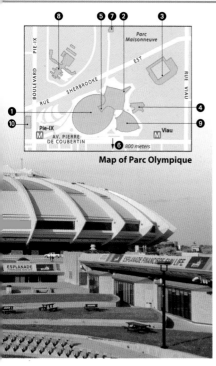

**Map of Parc Olympique**

❽ ❺ ❼ ❷ ❸

PIE-IX

BOULEVARD

Parc
Maisonneuve

EST

RUE

SHERBROOKE

RUE VIAU

❶

❹

❿

Viau

❾

Pie-IX

M

AV. PIERRE
DE COUBERTIN

M Viau

❻ 800 meters

## MAYOR JEAN DRAPEAU

Many agree that the enthusiasm of Jean Drapeau, the mayor of Montreal from 1954 to 1957 and again from 1960 to 1986, put Montreal on the international map. A lawyer by trade, he was passionate about his city, and while in office oversaw the building of the Métro subway system and the city's cultural venue Place des Arts, brought the World's Fair to town in 1967, and was largely responsible for the successful bid for the 1976 Olympic Games.

### ❼ Insectarium

Quebecer Georges Brossard, also known as "the Bug Man," roams the world collecting exotic insects, and then displays them in this riveting showcase *(see p50)*.

### ❽ Jardin Botanique

Founded in 1931 and covering nearly 185 acres (75 ha), the lush gardens were created by gifted horticulturist Henry Teuscher *(see pp20–21)*.

### Biodôme ❾

Home to ecological attractions, with indigenous plants, animals, and birds of the tropical forest **(right)**. It is closed for renovations until 2019 *(see p50)*.

### ❿ Musée Château Dufresne

The Gothic-inspired private residence was originally designed and constructed by Parisian architect Jules Rénard for Oscar and Marius Dufresne from 1915 to 1918. It now welcomes a variety of decorative and informative exhibitions.

## NEED TO KNOW

4141 Rue Pierre-de-Coubertin ▪ Métro Pie-IX ▪ (514) 252 4141 ▪ www.parc olympique.qc.ca

Adm to specific attractions

*Jardin Botanique*: 4101 Rue Sherbrooke Est; (514) 868 3000; www.espacepourlavie. ca; Mid-May–Oct: 9am–6pm daily, Nov–mid-May: 9am–5pm daily, closed Mon in Nov–May; Adm

▪ The best place to eat, for both price and atmosphere, is Café Olimpico in the Mile End district *(see p82)*.

▪ The "Since 1976" is a permanent and free exhibit in the Tour Montréal featuring artifacts, photos, and digital content about the history of the Parc Olympique.

# Jardin Botanique Features

**Tranquil Lac de Rêve**

### 1 Lac de Rêve

A lush domain in the center of the Chinese Gardens, where visitors can watch resident geese and ducks, find a comfortable area to relax, or just wander through the landscaped lake area surrounded by rock gardens, bridges, and peaceful areas for reflection.

### 2 First Nations Garden

The First Nations (native Canadians) celebrate their magical relationship with the plant kingdom within these gardens filled with interactive terminals, shows, and special events. The area is divided up into five different zones: hardwood and softwood forests, an exploration of Nordic life, an interpretation pavilion, and a gathering area.

### 3 Greenhouses

A series of greenhouses in the gardens, just past the entrance, provide enough humidity for various botanical environments to thrive.

Look out for the rainforest canopy, tropical medicinal plants, and beautiful, brightly colored orchids.

### 4 Sukiya Japanese Tea Pavilion

Honoring the traditional Japanese home, architect Hisato Hiraoka has gathered together the artistic ideals of Japanese society within this graceful structure. There is an art gallery, Zen and bonsai gardens, and an exhibition room.

### 5 Chinese Gardens

These traditionally designed Chinese gardens are one of the largest outside China, and are home to seven classical structures inspired by the Ming Dynasty.

**Lovingly nurtured Chinese Gardens**

### 6 Wu Yee-Sun Bonsai Collection

At any time of year, the captivating Wu Yee-Sun Collection of miniature bonsai trees is on permanent exhibit inside their greenhouse. This is one of the most impressive and largest collections of its kind in the world.

### 7 Frédéric Back Tree Pavilion

This remarkable interpretation center and interactive exhibition is laid out in four parts: Trees in our History, Anatomy and Growth, Trees and the Forest, and The Many Uses of Trees. This exhibit is in the northeast sector of the gardens.

**One of several greenhouses**

### 8 Mini train

Since the gardens are spread out over many acres, it's a good idea to take advantage of the popular mini train, which circulates continuously throughout the day along the paved pathways. Clearly marked areas within the gardens indicate where the bright red trains make regular stops for boarding or disembarking.

**A mini train in the gardens**

### 9 Libraries

There are two fascinating libraries situated within the gardens. The public library boasts an extensive children's section and there is also an academic library that is home to numerous scientific books, journals, and papers, including studies of botany.

### 10 Children's Highlights

Exciting and informative features in the garden are part of the ongoing effort to educate Montreal children and bring them closer to nature. Exhibitions that would interest kids include the Youth Gardens, Butterflies Go Free, the BuzzGround Playground, and the Insectarium *(see p50)*.

## HISTORY OF THE JARDIN BOTANIQUE

In 1931, Montreal's mayor, Camillien Houde, conceived of a master plan to put the unemployed to work by building the city's first botanical gardens. He hired architect Lucien Keroack to design the main building, and work began in the midst of a deep economic depression. Owing much to the Christian Brothers religious sect and particularly to Brother Marie-Victorin for his visionary concept, the team invited American landscape architect and botanist Henry Teuscher to establish the permanent collections and design the site. By 1938 the greenhouses were built and Montreal has enjoyed this rich horticultural domain ever since.

**TOP 10**
**FLORA IN THE JARDIN BOTANIQUE**

1 Aroids
2 Begonias
3 Bonsai and penjing
4 Ferns
5 Bromeliads
6 Cactuses and succulents
7 Cyads
8 Orchids
9 Lilacs and lotus
10 Gesneriads

**The Jardin Botanique** features an impressive collection of bonsai trees.

# 🔟 ⭐ Musée Pointe-à-Callière

Ascending like a sentinel from the confluence of the St Pierre and St Lawrence rivers, this National Historic Site honors the founding of Montreal at Place Royale. Within this landmark of stone and brushed steel are three sections: a chic building constructed on top of the ruins of older structures; the archaeological crypt; and the renovated Customs House. A self-guided tour system allows each visitor to explore at their own pace, but guides throughout the site will answer questions and bring the history of the city to life.

### 1 Éperon Building

Architect Dan S. Hanganu designed this edifice to create a building that is an exhibition in itself. The front door marks the spot of the first shelter in Ville-Marie (1642).

### 2 Tales of a City

This 18-minute voyage through the discovery of Montreal is an inspired introduction to the museum, enchanting visitors and setting the stage for a memorable visit.

### 3 Where Montreal Began

This exhibition (right) represents more than 600 years of local history, from Amerindian times to the present day.

The Musée Pointe-à-Callière site

### 4 First Catholic Cemetery in North America

Residents from the very earliest days of the original fortification created a cemetery under Place Royale. When the museum excavated the site, the discovery resulted in this fascinating exhibit (left).

### 5 Underground Vaulted Conduit

Montreal's earliest sewer and plumbing system, dating from the 18th century, can be seen in this network of conduits, beneath a cobblestoned walkway. Another excavation revealed the St Pierre River.

**Plan of Musée Pointe-à-Callière**

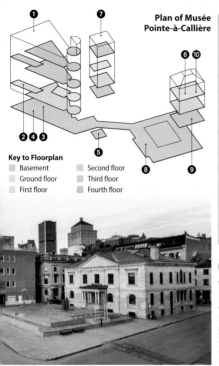

**Key to Floorplan**
- Basement
- Ground floor
- First floor
- Second floor
- Third floor
- Fourth floor

### HISTORY OF THE MUSEUM

In 1642 Paul de Chomedey, Sieur de Maisonneuve, founded the settlement of Ville-Marie, now Montreal, on this site. More than 350 years later, a series of excavations unearthed the way of life for these newcomers to Nouvelle-France and Musée Pointe-à-Callière opened with over one million artifacts on display. A permanent archaeological dig is now in place in the area.

### NEED TO KNOW

**MAP K3** ■ 350 Place Royale at Rue de la Commune ■ (514) 872 9150 ■ www.pacmusee.qc.ca

**Open** 10am–5pm Tue–Fri, 11am–5pm Sat & Sun

Adm $22 adults; $19 senior citizens; $13 students (13–17); $8 children; under-5s free

■ One of the best views in all of Vieux-Montréal is available from L'Arrivage Bistro, on the top level of the museum. It serves great French cuisine, and has a reasonably priced table d'hôte menu at lunch.

### 6 Market Day, 1750

This interactive fresco is set in the remains of the main gate that led to the marketplace in 1750. Visitors can see virtual figures and play out scenes from their lives.

### 8 Models At Your Feet

Virtual technology bridges past with present here. Meet historic figures, hear archaeological explanations, and view five centuries of artifacts under glass beneath your feet.

### 9 A Customs House and its Architect

Montreal's old Customs House, built between 1836 and 1837, is a Neo-Classical building designed by John Ostell. It has been carefully renovated to its original state and houses a permanent exhibition.

### 10 Montreal Love Stories

This series of intimate portraits of the city draws on photographs, videos, and first-hand accounts of Montrealers.

### 7 Youville Pumping Station Interpretation Center

Across from the museum an old pumping station **(above)** has exhibits on science and technology.

# TOP 10 ★ Musée des Beaux-Arts de Montréal

One of the most impressive museums in North America dominates both sides of Rue Sherbrooke Ouest. It began life in 1860, when a group of collectors set up the Art Association of Montreal to present exhibitions, establish an art school, assemble a permanent collection of paintings, and develop an art library. They eventually constructed the Michal and Renata Hornstein Pavilion, to house Old Masters and contemporary works. In 1991, the museum expanded into the Jean-Noël Desmarais Pavilion.

**1 Venice, Looking out over the Lagoon**
A voyeur of the human landscape, Morrice is known for his departure from centuries of art tradition and for his philosophy of painting for painting's sake, seen in this work.

**2 Portrait of the Lawyer Hugo Simons**
Otto Dix's artistic freedom is evident in this 1929 portrait of lawyer Hugo Simons. The image, bathed in reddish-copper tones, shows Dix's wish to portray his subjects' souls in his works.

**3 Apelles Painting the Portrait of Campaspe**
Italian artist Tiepolo uses the unusual technique of a painting-within-a-painting in this 1726 work (above). Notice the artwork hanging on the wall of the studio, one of Tiepolo's own, entitled *The Bronze Serpent*.

**4 Octobre**
An example of James Tissot's control and mastery of space, this 1877 allegorical work is of his muse and mistress Kathleen Irene Newton (left).

**5 Judith with the Head of Holofernes, Dido**
In these two paintings (1500), Andrea Mantegna demonstrates typical Renaissance traits: absence of emotion, knowledge of anatomy, and determinism of line.

**6 Portrait of a Young Woman**
A combined use of light, color, texture, and setting brings a feeling of intimacy to this 1665 Rembrandt work (above).

### 10 The Tribute Money
Philippe de Champaigne's 1655 work portrays the Biblical tale of the Pharisees in this dramatic religious painting. The figure on the right is said to be a self-portrait **(left)**.

### 7 The Wheel
Montreal's best-known contemporary painter, Jean-Paul Riopelle, lets his spatula work its magic on this canvas (1954–5), creating a mosaic of elements, colors, and tones.

### 8 The Black Star
Paul-Émile Borduas attended the École des Beaux-Arts in Montreal. This 1957 painting won a posthumous Guggenheim award in 1960 as the best Canadian painting in a New York gallery; the work has now returned to the artist's home town.

### 9 Mauve Twilight
Painted in 1921, this work is an evocative impression of winter by one of Quebec's most loved artists, Ozias Leduc. His ability to capture the light of dusk here confirms his talent for perfectly representing the provincial landscape.

**Key to Floorplan**
- Level 4
- Level 3
- Level S2

Judith with the Head of Holofernes, Dido **5**

The Tribute Money **10**

Octobre **4**

Portrait of a Young Woman **6**

Venice, Looking out over the Lagoon **1**

Apelles Painting the Portrait of Campaspe **3**

Portrait of the Lawyer Hugo Simons **2**

The Black Star **8**

The Wheel **7**

Mauve Twilight **9**

---

**NEED TO KNOW**

**MAP C3** ▪ (514) 285 2000 ▪ 1339–80 Rue Sherbrooke Ouest ▪ www.mbam.qc.ca

**Open** 10am–5pm Tue & Thu–Sun, 10am–9pm Wed

▪ On-site Le Beaux-Arts restaurant serves delicious but expensive French bistro cuisine *(see p74)*, but there is also the inexpensive Petit Café in the same area of the Jean-Noël Desmarais Pavilion.

**Museum Guide**
There are five pavilions that make up the museum; the Michal and Renata Hornstein Pavilion (world cultures), which contains the Liliane and David M. Stewart Pavilion featuring decorative arts. The Jean-Noël Desmarais Pavilion, connected via a tunnel from Level S2, features international art. The Claire and Marc Bourgie Pavilion features Canadian and Quebec art, and the Michal and Renata Hornstein Pavilion for Peace is devoted to the world's artistic heritage.

---

*Following pages* Lac de Rêve, Jardin Botanique, Montreal

# TOP 10 ⭐ La Citadelle, Quebec City

Set atop Cap Diamant, this installation of 24 buildings is the largest military fortification in North America. Overlooking the St Lawrence River, the site was begun by the French in 1693, but much of the star-shaped battlement seen today was constructed by the British between 1820 and 1850, built to defend the city from possible invasion from the United States in the 19th century. The fort is home to the Royal 22nd Regiment of the Canadian Armed Forces and daily military spectacles are staged for visitors during the summer.

## Changing of the Guard ①

One of the most enjoyable military exercises **(right)** involves precision marching with a musical escort. It is headed by Batisse the goat, the regiment's mascot.

## ② Dalhousie Gate

Named in honor of 13th-century Castle Dalhousie in Scotland, this formal entrance provides general access to La Citadelle and is the point at which processions and parades enter the grounds **(above)**.

## ③ Fortifications

The impressive fortress **(right)** contains all of the most important elements for a strong military installation: height over the enemy, 360-degree visibility, difficult access, and durability. Although it has all of this to its advantage, La Citadelle has never, in fact, been attacked by an enemy.

## ④ Outer Walls

In 1820, under the British Lieutenant-Colonel Elias Walker Durnford, building of the outer walls of the polygon structure began. No one could access the Great Lakes or the Atlantic Ocean without coming under the watchful eye of La Citadelle's forces.

## ⑤ Museums

The collections unveiled in the two museums located here include everyday items used by soldiers over the centuries, a collection of rare military documents, ceremonial uniforms, antique armaments, precious art, and many other eclectic items.

**Plan of La Citadelle**

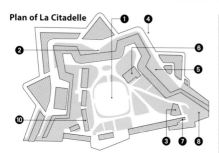

### 8 Redoubt

Tucked away into sections of the fieldstone walls, cannons protect their flanks without the need for backup support.

### 9 Firing of the Cannon

The firing of the cannon is an exciting event that takes place at the Citadelle every day at noon. It's a fine illustration of the military might the fort once displayed.

### 6 Chapel

Since army life requires long periods of working far from home, efforts were made to include elements of daily life at the fortification, including a chapel.

### 7 Governor-General's Residence

Since 1872, the Governor General has resided in this 153-room home during the summer months.

**NEED TO KNOW**

**MAP L6** ■ 1 Côte de la Citadelle
■ (418) 694 2815
■ www.lacitadelle.qc.ca

**Open** daily

Adm $16 adults, $14 students and senior citizens, $6 youth, $36 families (under-10s free)

■ Snacks are available at the on-site Café Batisse, although you are also welcome to bring a picnic.

■ The Changing of the Guard takes place daily at 10am from late June to September and lasts about 35 minutes.

### 10 Barracks

A large part of the site is given over to housing the troops. Tanks used in past battles by the regiment are also on display **(above)**.

# TOP 10 ⭐ Musée de la Civilisation de Québec

Few museums in the world receive the kind of rave reviews given to the MCQ. The exhibitions (two of which are permanent) cover history, culture, sports, science, and intellectual and esoteric themes in a range of interactive ways that entertain and educate visitors. Designed by the celebrated architect Moshe Safdie, creator of Ottawa's National Gallery, the MCQ incorporates the Musée de l'Amérique Francophone, the Maison Historique Chevalier, and the Séminaire de Québec, to produce this vibrant look at local life in all its facets. The main entrance is at the Rue Dalhousie site.

### 1 Séminaire de Québec

Three superb exhibitions in the seminary form the largest religious collection in North America. The artifacts document the early religious education of the city.

### 2 The Chapel of the Séminaire de Québec

Information about Catholic rites and church decoration can be found inside the chapel.

### 3 Musée de l'Amérique Francophone

Exhibitions include the colonial history of North America, Francophone culture in North America, and local arts and crafts.

### 4 Joseph the Boarder

An enchanting interactive presentation, located in the Jérôme-Demers Pavilion, recalls daily life in Le Petit Séminaire de Québec for "Joseph," a typical waif in the early days of Nouvelle-France.

**Musée de la civilisation**

### 5 People of Québec... Then and Now

Visitors can relive 400 years of Quebec's history, meeting figures and admiring objects from yesterday and connecting to a past that is still shaping the events of today **(right)**.

---

**NEED TO KNOW**

**MAP M4** ■ 85 Rue Dalhousie, Basse-Ville, Québec City
■ (418) 643 2158
■ www.mcq.org

**Open** 10am–5pm Tue–Sun; mid-Jun–Labor Day: 10am–5pm daily

Adm over-30s $17, 18–30 $11, 12–17 $6, families $38, under-11s free

■ Good food at a reasonable price is found at the on-site Café 47 near the coat-check area.

■ Do not try to see everything the MCQ offers at their three locations in one day. For a more enjoyable experience, plan to attend only those parts that you are most interested in.

### 7 Encounter with First Nations

This magnificent exhibition of First Nations' treasures **(left)** has over 500 objects displayed covering the history of the native Canadians.

### 8 Make Way for the Middle Ages

Based around the workings of a medieval French village, this costume workshop explores how certain aspects of life in the Middle Ages have influenced how we live in the modern age.

**SEPARATISM**

Ever since the British made an offer in 1848 to allow the French to maintain their language within an English-speaking domain, the relationship between what would become the nation of Canada and the province of Quebec has been fraught with mistrust. As Canada and Quebec repeatedly experienced political deadlock, separatist sentiment grew. Many Québécois feel that their province is distinct from the rest of Canada, and so would be better off as a separate nation. In 1980 and 1995, referendums were held on whether to separate, and both times the vote was a narrow "no."

### 9 Église Notre-Dame-des-Victoires

Originally built in 1687, this French colonial stone church is the city's oldest. It was mostly destroyed by British bombs in 1759 but has since been restored several times *(see p94)*.

### 10 Maison Historique Chevalier

Jean-Baptiste Chevalier's 18th-century home **(below)** allows visitors to see what life was like here over the last three centuries.

**Map of Museum Sites**

### 6 Place-Royale

Life as it was in Nouvelle-France comes alive at Place-Royale; historic events are held on the site of the first settlement.

# TOP 10 ⭐ Basilique Sainte-Anne-de-Beaupré

One of the oldest pilgrimage sites in North America began life in 1658 as a shrine to this patron saint of Québec and was established as a basilica in 1887. The present church, started in 1923 but completed in 1963, has a striking interior with sumptuous decoration. Medical aids stacked beside the medieval-style entrance are testimony to the healing powers associated with the basilica. Stunning religious statues frame the entrance and line the luxurious gardens.

### 1 Candlelight Processions

It is common to witness evening candlelight processions honoring saints and religious holidays; those on July 25 and 26 celebrate Ste Anne.

### 2 Stained-Glass Windows

Considered by some to be the most beautiful since the Middle Ages, these dazzling 240 stained-glass windows **(above)** depict moments in the life of Ste Anne. The centerpiece is a huge oval window flooding light into the nave.

The impressive nave

### 3 Medieval Architecture

A five-nave towered church **(left)** blends imposing Gothic architecture with Romanesque details previously unseen in Québec Province.

### 4 Memorial Chapel

This votive chapel, built in 1878 to commemorate the original church on this site, contains religious memorabilia, rare documents, and artifacts.

**NEED TO KNOW**

**MAP P3** ▪ 10018 Ave Royale, Sainte-Anne-de-Beaupré ▪ (418) 827 3781 ▪ www.sanctuairesainte anne.org

**Open** daily

▪ To get a wonderful view of the church complex and the river, take a 10-minute walk from the gardens down the Rue de la Sanctuaire toward the Île d'Orleans Channel to the Quai de la Paix. This is a great spot to take photos.

▪ Call ahead to check the opening hours for specific sites or for information regarding any special celebrations or festivities taking place, since the crowds can be an impediment to enjoying the site.

**Plan of Basilique Sainte-Anne-de-Beaupré**

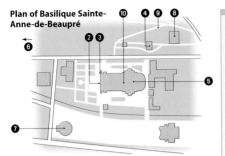

### 9 Way of the Cross Bronzes

Life-size statues line the hillside trail beside the basilica. Honoring saints and Apostles, these add a Renaissance feeling to the grounds **(below)**.

### 5 St Augustin

Thomas Baillairgé continued his family's legacy as a religious decorator by carving pieces for the basilica, including an impressive statue of St Augustin.

### 8 Scala Santa

A wonderful little chapel constructed in 1891 includes a remarkable stairway venerating the one Jesus ascended to face condemnation by Pontius Pilate.

### 10 Relics

Three notable relics are housed in the Basilica - partial finger bones and two sets of forearm bones, all supposedly from Saint Anne.

### 6 Atelier Paré

This woodcarver's workshop is worth a visit to see the artisan at work creating pieces for the basilica.

### Cyclorama de Jérusalem 7

This hexagonal building **(right)** houses the world's largest circular painting, created in Munich from 1878 to 1882. It transfixes visitors with its panorama of the Holy Land.

# ⭐ Île d'Orléans

A haven of greenery and tranquility, Île d'Orléans was one of the first European settlements in the New World. Ever since Jacques Cartier arrived here in 1535, the six parishes along this 18-mile (30-km) island have maintained many of the French traditions of the first settlers, and over 600 heritage buildings present a preserved architectural gem. Rich with fertile soil, the island produces an abundance of local food that draws thousands of visitors every year.

**1 Île de Bacchus**
When Jacques Cartier found wild grape vines here he named it Île de Bacchus after the Greek god of wine, then changed the name to honor the Duke of Orleans.

**2 Domaine Steinbach**
Domaine Steinbach, in St-Pierre, welcomes visitors for organic cider tastings, and also makes vinegar and mustards.

The town of St-Jean on Île d'Orléans

### NEED TO KNOW

**MAP P3** ■ Dufferin-Montmorency highway 440

*Bureau d'information touristique:*
490 côte du Pont, St-Pierre-de-l'Île-d'Orléans; (418) 828 9411; www.iledorleans.com

■ Auberge Restaurant Le Canard Huppé in St-Laurent *(2198 chemin Royal; 1-800-838 2292)* offers fine cuisine. They have B&B rooms, should you want to stay. There are also many other B&Bs across the island.

■ The tranquility here makes it a perfect spot to rent a bicycle, follow the walking guide from the Interpretation Center, or enjoy a picnic beside the river.

**3 Montmorency Falls**
Higher than Niagara Falls, Montmorency Falls **(below)** are a dramatic sight before you cross the bridge onto the island *(see p102)*.

**4 Auberge la Goéliche**
Located in the lovely community of Ste-Pétronille, the Auberge la Goéliche offers guests old-world hospitality, food, and ambiance.

### 6 Manoir Mauvide-Genest

This 1734 manor **(left)** is one of the oldest buildings in the province and a fine example of rural architecture from the 18th century. There's a small on-site museum and a seasonal market.

### 7 Horatio Walker Studio

The Canadian landscape artist Horatio Walker was a resident of the island, and his studio has been preserved in Ste-Pétronille on the street renamed in his honor. His legacy continues in the work of other island painters such as Horace Champagne.

---

**FÉLIX LECLERC**

No mention of Île d'Orléans would be complete without reference to the spirit of the province at large, as it was embodied in the artistry of Félix Leclerc (1914–88). The legacy of this prolific singer, songwriter, poet, and playwright *(see p42)*, and his ability to perfectly express the Québécois sensibility is honored at L'Espace Félix-Leclerc *(1214 chemin Royal, St-Pierre; open daily)* where there is a permanent exhibition on his work, as well as a library and a gift shop.

---

**Map of Île d'Orléans**

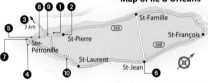

St-Famille

St-François

St-Pierre

3 km

Ste-Pétronille

St-Laurent

St-Jean

### 5 Chocolaterie de l'Île d'Orléans

Ste-Pétronille is home to the most wonderful chocolate-maker in the province **(below)**, who also sells delicious home-made ice cream, jellies, and other edible goodies. It houses an interpretation center that explains the process of creating chocolate.

### 8 Le Vignoble Ste-Pétronille

With an incredible view across the St Lawrence River to Montmorency Falls, this 60-acre vineyard **(right)** is an excellent example of a quality, cold-weather grape-bearing plantation that creates popular red, white, and rosé wines.

### 9 Bureau d'accueil Touristique

The island's friendly tourist office offers excellent maps, brochures, audio guides, and local advice on where to stay and what to do.

### 10 La Forge-à-Pique-Assaut

The forge offers a fascinating opportunity to look inside a blacksmith's workshop. See artisan Guy Bel at work, as he continues to labor here, admirably maintaining traditional metal-working techniques.

# 🔟 ⭐ Les Laurentides

Les Laurentides (the Laurentians) are part of a shield of forested peaks enclosed by the Ottawa, St Lawrence, and Saguenay rivers, and are known for their ski slopes, which roll into sight one hour north of Montreal. First Nations relics indicate Amerindian settlements here over 4,000 years ago. Since the 19th century the region has been a rich agricultural zone and is famous for fishing in its 6,000 lakes and ponds. Visitors can enjoy the historic Francophone villages, numerous cycling and hiking trails in summer, and luxury ski resorts in winter.

### 1 St-Sauveur-des-Monts
Downhill skiing is the draw here in winter, but in summer the artisans' shops, restaurants, and galleries tempt visitors to town **(below)**.

### 3 Mont-Rolland
The historic homes in this laid-back village were built to house workers of the Rolland Mill, which was once the main employer of this forested domain.

### 2 Ste-Adèle
Spectacular outdoor recreation within easy reach of Montreal attracted the first tourist train to Ste-Adèle in 1891, and the town continues to welcome ski enthusiasts to the challenging slopes today.

### 4 Ville d'Estérel
A lush, rolling area including Ste-Marguerite-du-Lac-Masson, the village where renowned artist Jean-Paul Riopelle painted for many years. The area was originally developed by a Belgian aristocrat in the 1930s.

### 5 Val-Morin
Located along the P'tit Train du Nord cycle path, this tiny Francophone village beguiles visitors as the trail meanders around Lac Raymond. Skiers can take to the slopes at the ski resort Belle Neige.

**NEED TO KNOW**

**MAP N5**

*Maison de Tourisme de Laurentides:* Port du Nord, Exit 51, Highway 15; (450) 224 7007; www.laurentides.com

■ Visit the busy La Table des Gourmets in Val-David for unpretentious yet sophisticated French food. The eatery is run by Breton-born chef, Thierry Rouyé, and his wife, Pascale.

■ Reasonably priced and comfortable log cabins are available on a first-come-first-served basis inside the Parc National de Mont-Tremblant *(418-890 6527)*.

### 6 St-Jovite
The gateway to the Mont-Tremblant commercial district, the village of St-Jovite **(left)** offers visitors boutiques and traditional Québécois restaurants. Visit the palatial Monastère des Apôtres de l'Amour Infini just east of town.

### 7 Ste-Agathe-des-Monts
With its fishing, swimming, and skiing, Ste-Agathe-des-Monts became the first resort in Les Laurentides over 100 years ago.

#### "JACKRABBIT" JOHANNSEN
Born in Norway in 1875, Herman "Jackrabbit" Johannsen settled in the Montreal area with his wife and children in 1928. First Nations residents apparently gave him his nickname after watching him moving mysteriously and swiftly across the snow. This remarkable man, who lived an active outdoor life until the age of 111, put the Laurentian Mountains on the global ski map and was responsible for bringing cross-country skiing to Canada.

### 9 Parc National du Mont-Tremblant
The second largest of an awe-inspiring list of provincial parks **(left)**, it provides a haven for black bears, white-tailed deer, moose, wolves, raccoons, and over 200 species of birds. Outdoor activities include canoeing, fishing, and cross-country skiing.

### 8 Val-David
An enthralling town peppered with art galleries, which hosts music and poetry festivals, and is known for its rock climbing culture.

### Map of Les Laurentides

### 10 Mont Tremblant
This is the highest peak in Les Laurentides at over 900 m (2,950 ft) and one of the most popular ski resorts in North America. Spas, shops, excellent dining, and live entertainment all add to the appeal **(above)**.

# The Top 10
# of Everything

The Neo-Classical Marché
Bonsecours, Montreal

# 🔟 Moments in History

Iroquoian settlement on the shores of the St Lawrence River

### 1 First Nations

Iroquoian and nomadic Algonquian peoples had lived in Quebec for thousands of years when the first Europeans arrived. "Kebec" is an Algonquian word meaning "place where the river narrows."

### 2 Jacques Cartier

The French explorer Jacques Cartier followed Basque fishing routes up the St Lawrence River, claiming "discovery" of Canada for King François I of France in 1534. He continued up the river in 1535 to land at the village of Hochelaga, where he named its mountain Mont-Royal (see pp12–13).

### 3 Samuel de Champlain

French settlement began in 1608 when Samuel de Champlain (1567–1635) arrived in the region. The position of Quebec City, protected atop Cap Diamant, became the driving force of the settlement, together with the newly found riches of the fur trade.

The siege of Quebec City, 1759

### 4 British Takeover

The struggle between the French and British in Europe continued in the New World. Eventually, in 1759 after a summer-long stand-off, British General James Wolfe won claim to the province during the 30-minute siege of Quebec City on the Plains of Abraham. However, in 1774 the French were granted language and religion rights (see p31).

### 5 The Creation of Canada

After the Constitutional Act (1791) separated the colony into Upper Canada (southern Ontario) and Lower Canada (southern Quebec), British Lord Durham was sent to solve the ongoing problems between the English and French halves. He declared the Union Act of 1841, which fused the two sides under a single English-speaking parliament and effectively marginalized the French. By 1848, the English were forced to accept the use of French in order to avoid a backlash. On July 1, 1867, Quebec and Ontario joined with Nova Scotia and New Brunswick to form the Dominion of Canada, a federated kingdom in its own right.

### 6 The Dark Years

Well into the 20th century the Roman Catholic church held considerable political sway in Quebec. Maurice Duplessis' right-wing Union Nationale (1936–9 and 1944–59) used the church's moral influence to gain votes and accepted $100-million-worth of graft.

### 7 The Quiet Revolution

The collusion of church and state led to widespread resentment among Québécois. With the death of Duplessis, liberal sentiment grew. In 1960, the Liberal Party was elected, leading to province-wide social reforms and economic development.

### 8 The October Crisis

Political deadlock with Canada increased support for the separatist movement among Québécois. In October 1970 the radical separatist Front de Libération du Québec (FLQ) kidnapped two high-ranking politicians, murdering one of them.

**René Lévesque, ex-leader of the PQ**

### 9 Parti Québécois

René Lévesque's separatist Parti Québécois (PQ) was in power from 1976 to 1985 and ensured French-language dominance in Quebec with Bill 101, alarming the province's Anglophone minority.

### 10 Oui ou Non?

Opinion on whether Quebec should split from Canada has evolved over the years. In a 1995 referendum held by the PQ, just 50.5 percent voted "no." Since then, support has fallen as the PQ drops in and out of power.

---

**TOP 10 MONUMENTS**

**De Maisonneuve Monument**

**1 De Maisonneuve Monument**
MAP K2
The Sieur de Maisonneuve ambushed by Iroquois stands at place d'Armes.

**2 Croix du Parc du Mont-Royal**
The Sieur de Maisonneuve erected a cross in 1643 after the Ville-Marie settlement survived floods (see p12).

**3 Place Royale**
In 1642 settlers built a stockade where Montreal was founded (see p44).

**4 Nelson Monument**
MAP L3 ▪ Place Jacques-Cartier
Controversially erected in 1809 to celebrate victory over the French at the Battle of Trafalgar.

**5 Saint Brother André**
MAP H2 ▪ Blvd Réne-Lévesque Ouest
A bronze monument commemorates the founder of the Oratoire St-Joseph (see pp14–15).

**6 La Foule Illuminée**
MAP J1 ▪ Ave McGill College
This sculpture by Raymond Masson fronts the Banque Nationale de Paris.

**7 James McGill**
MAP J1 ▪ Ave McGill College
A monument dedicated to the university's founder.

**8 Monument George-Étienne Cartier**
Montreal's largest monument is the setting for the Tam-Tam Festival (see p13).

**9 Wolfe-Montcalm Monument**
MAP L5 ▪ Parc des Gouverneurs
Commemorating the French and English generals.

**10 Jardins Jeanne d'Arc**
MAP J6
An equestrian memorial of the French heroine is surrounded by gardens.

# TOP 10 Cultural Québécois

**Novelist Gabrielle Roy**

### 1 Gabrielle Roy
Born in Manitoba to a French mother, and the youngest of 11 children, Roy (1909–83) escaped her family's poverty and moved to Quebec in 1939, where she began her career as a respected and prolific French-speaking novelist. Her first work, *Bonheur d'occasion (The Tin Flute)*, was published in 1945, winning her the Prix Fémina award and the first of three coveted Governor General's awards.

### 2 Émile Nelligan
Nelligan (1879–1941) was a romantic figurehead who ushered French-Canadian poetry into a new epoch and is revered by Quebecers as their beloved literary spokesman. In 1897 Nelligan joined the École Littéraire de Montréal and caused a triumphant public reaction to the reading of his poem "La Romance du Vin." In his later years Nelligan's sanity deteriorated and he spent his last days in an asylum.

### 3 Mary Travers
Travers (1894–1941), born to an impoverished family on the Gaspé Peninsula, was a natural entertainer and began her career at family soirées playing jigs on the fiddle and spoons. Known as "La Bolduc," she rose to fame during the Great Depression to become the first popular singer-songwriter from Quebec. Today, a new generation of Quebecers enjoys her musical traditions.

### 4 Paul-Émile Borduas
The painter Borduas (1905–60) is one of Quebec's most legendary artists and also one of its greatest political activists. Born in St-Hilaire, just outside Montreal, he made his name when he criticized the established social and political norms in 1948 by writing a scathing manifesto entitled *Refus Global*. He was a founding member of the abstract Automatistes school of art, which included Jean-Paul Riopelle.

### 5 Félix Leclerc
Leclerc (1914–88) worked as a radio announcer, actor, and comedian, but he is probably best remembered as a consummate storyteller, singer, and songwriter, penning works about the Canadian countryside, solitude, and love. His monument is found on Île d'Orléans, and a statue of him has been erected in his honor in Parc Lafontaine in Montreal (see p46).

### 6 Oscar Peterson
Peterson (1925–2007) entered an amateur talent contest aged 14 in his home town of Montreal – an event that he went on to win and

**Oscar Peterson receiving a Grammy**

**A magical performance from circus troupe Cirque du Soleil**

which inspired him to leave high school and dedicate his life to jazz. However his father only gave him permission to do so providing he worked to become the best jazz pianist in the world. Peterson succeeded beyond anyone's imagination: five unequalled decades of recordings are a testament to his virtuosity and have made him one of the greats of this musical genre.

### 7 Mordecai Richler

The Montreal novelist, essayist, and critic (1931–2001) was known for his sarcastic wit and biting opposition to Quebec's separatist elements. His most popular book, *The Apprenticeship of Duddy Kravitz* (1959), was adapted for film, launching Richard Dreyfuss to Hollywood stardom in 1974. Richler is best known for writing about greed and the human condition, as in *St Urbain's Horseman* (1971) and *Barney's Version* (1997), but he also wrote a number of humorous essays.

### 8 Robert Lepage

The first North American to direct a Shakespeare play at London's Royal National Theatre, Lepage (b.1957) is one of the most successful and daring writer/directors in the visual-arts world. He has won every available Canadian award for his brilliant theatrical staging and continues to expand his creativity as a filmmaker.

### 9 Cirque du Soleil

This circus troupe was born as street performers in Baie-St-Paul, northeast of Quebec City. Employing a mix of stunning acrobatics, dazzling costumes, and inventive music, Cirque has become the most famous circus in the world. Headquartered in Montreal, Cirque has touring and resident shows in cities around the globe, most evident in Las Vegas.

**Céline Dion in concert**

### 10 Céline Dion

Dion (b.1968) was born into a musical family in Charlemagne. A demo tape made at 12 years old led to an agent, the late René Angélil, a recording contract, and eventually to her and Angélil's marriage. Today, Dion is one of the greatest Canadian artists in history, with record sales of over 250 million copies worldwide.

# 🔟 Historic Sites

**Marché Bonsecours, one of Canada's finest heritage buildings**

## 1 Marché Bonsecours, Montreal

This beautiful Neo-Classical domed structure was once home to Canada's parliament but is today used variously as a produce market, art gallery, concert venue, reception hall, and shopping mall, and is home to Quebec Crafts Council. The symmetrical gem of Vieux-Montréal features a Greek Revival portico and cast-iron columns made in the early 1800s *(see p62)*.

## 2 La Citadelle, Quebec City

The colossal fortification was originally built by Royal Engineer Josué Dubois Berthelot de Beaucours in 1693. The complete star-shaped bastion seen today, however, is primarily the work of English Colonel Elias Durnford, constructed between 1820 and 1832 *(see pp28–9)*.

## 3 Basilique Notre-Dame, Montreal

Once the largest church in North America, the imposing Gothic towers of the cathedral loom over Place d'Armes. The inside has a decorative nave composed of stained-glass windows, hand-carved wooden statues, ornate goldleaf trimmings, and paintings *(see pp16–17)*.

## 4 Place Royale, Montreal
MAP K3

Montreal's oldest public square (1657) is located on the site where the city was originally founded in 1642. Small and easy to overlook, the square features the Pointe-à-Callière museum *(see pp22–3)*, a gift shop, and outdoor events. The residence of Louis-Hector Callière, a French governor, was also once located here, as was the 19th-century Royal Insurance Building and Montreal's first Customs House.

## 5 Château Ramezay, Montreal

An elegant heritage museum sits across the street from the Hôtel de Ville in an 18th-century former

**Elegant interior of Château Ramezay**

governor's home. Artifacts from Amerindian societies through to the arrival of British and French colonizers up to 1900 are on display. The gift shop has unique souvenirs and the comfortable café terrace faces onto the Jardins du Gouverneur and Place Jacques-Cartier *(see p62)*.

### 6 Sir George-Étienne-Cartier National Historic Site, Montreal

**Exhibit at Sir George-Étienne-Cartier National Historic Site**

A Victorian home, restored by Parks Canada as a National Historic Site, contains marvelous interactive exhibitions inviting visitors into a typical 19th-century parlor. Enjoy theatrical re-enactments portrayed in shows such as "A Victorian Christmas," "A Servant Confides," and "Elegance and Propriety: Etiquette at the Cartiers," all of which offer a fascinating insight into the lives once lived here *(see p63)*.

### 7 Place Jacques-Cartier, Montreal

The magnetic center of Vieux-Montréal, this square offers a variety of stores, clubs and restaurants, while being enlivened by street performers and horse-drawn *calèche* rides. This is a wonderful spot to arrange meetings, take breaks from sightseeing, sit in the sun with a good book, or simply people-watch. Look out for an entertaining troupe called the Old Montreal Ghost Trail located just south of the square, who offer fascinating tours of the city's eerier past *(see p62)*.

### 8 Hôtel de Ville, Montreal

While visiting Montreal's World Fair in 1967, French president Charles de Gaulle made history from the balcony of this building by announcing *"Vive le Québec – Vive le Québec Libre!"* ("Long Live Quebec – Long Live Free Quebec"), proving his support for the province's separation from the rest of Canada *(see p31)*. Sign up for a guided tour to enjoy fully the grace of this historic town hall built in the Second Empire style *(see p61)*.

### 9 Parc des Champs-de-Bataille, Quebec City

This park commemorates the Battle of the Plains of Abraham, in which the generals of both sides, English General Wolfe and French General Montcalm, died during a fierce engagement lasting only 30 minutes *(see p40)*. The element of surprise was on the side of the British as no army had ever before managed to scale the Cap Diamant escarpment. A visit to the Plains of Abraham Museum at 835 Rue Wilfrid-Laurier will explain more on this important event and its consequences for Canadian history *(see p94)*.

**Iconic Château Frontenac**

### 10 Château Frontenac, Quebec City

Among the most photographed hotels in the world, this elegant château poses majestically on the heights of Haute-Ville. Built by railroad tycoon Cornelius Van Horne, this hotel was the first to belong to the Canadian Pacific railroad empire *(see p112)*.

#  Parks and Waterways

### ① Pôle-des-Rapides
**MAP P6**

This historic area originated from the drama of the Lachine Rapids, which prevented early explorers, settlers, traders, and the military from continuing farther west. It now includes the communities of Lachine, LaSalle, and Verdun, minutes from downtown Montreal. Boasting the most popular cycle path in Canada and 60 miles (100 km) of trails, the district is also home to the Fur Trade at Lachine National Historic Site.

**Urban green space of Parc Lafontaine**

### ② Parc du Mont-Royal, Montreal

The largest and most inviting natural playground in Montreal is a year-round magnet for outdoor sports enthusiasts as well as leisure and relaxation buffs. Parc du Mont-Royal boasts a wealth of wildlife and bird species, as well as a lake, streams, hiking paths, summer cycling, and winter cross-country skiing trails, lookouts, an interpretation center, and a wonderful collection of original sculptures (see pp12–13).

### ③ Parc Maisonneuve, Montreal
**Métro Viau**

Situated within the Parc Olympique area (see pp18–19), this huge chunk of greenery provide fun and leisure in the east of the city. Facilities include a nine-hole golf course in summer and a winter ice-skating rink.

### ④ Parc Lafontaine, Montreal
**MAP E2**

On the site of an old military armament range, attractive tree-lined pathways and shady spots are a perfect setting for many cultural events, celebrations, and community activities throughout the year. The park is a friendly neighborhood expanse containing a duck pond, cultural center, concert venue, and monuments honoring Québécois figures such as Félix Leclerc.

### ⑤ Parc Jean-Drapeau, Montreal
**MAP F5**

Parc Jean-Drapeau is made up of Île Sainte-Hélène and Île Notre-Dame. Most visitors come here to attend

**Biosphère, Parc Jean-Drapeau**

the amusement park or the numerous festivals and fireworks displays held throughout the year.

### 6 Parc des Champs-de-Bataille, Quebec City

This is the city's largest and most scenic park. With over 250 acres (100 ha) of undulating hills and the St Lawrence River on the horizon, it's hard to believe that beautiful Battlefields Park has such a harsh military history. It was the site of the famed Battle of the Plains of Abraham in 1759, the events of which formed British Canada *(see p94)*.

**Parc des Champs-de-Bataille**

### 7 Parc de la Francophonie, Quebec City

MAP K6

Created to commemorate the cultural alliance of 84 French-speaking governments and states, this peaceful park is dotted with ponds and fountains. It stands in stark contrast to the politically active area in which it lies, right beside the parliament building. This historic area was formerly known as Quartier St-Louis.

### 8 Parc du Cavalier du Moulin, Quebec City

MAP L5

At the western end of Rue Mont-Carmel sits a delightful park, where poets, lovers, and tourists enjoy the remarkable view of Avenue Sainte-Geneviève, the Chalmers-Wesley United Church, Hôtel du Parlement, La Citadelle, and the striking houses standing on Rue Saint-Louis.

### 9 Parc Montmorency, Quebec City

MAP M5

At this magnificent vantage point, overlooking the St Lawrence River, Alfred Laliberté, a Montreal sculptor, has created bronze memorials to many famous Canadians, including one of Sir George-Étienne Cartier, whose signature is on the Confederation Act of 1867. From here there are great views of the Séminaire de Québec.

### 10 Square Dorchester and Place du Canada, Montreal

MAP H2

This gracious square was the Catholic cemetery from 1798 to 1854 and is surrounded by elegant churches and buildings. Highlighted by the Sun Life Building on its east side, once the largest structure in the British Commonwealth, Square Dorchester contains numerous monuments, including one of the first French Canadian prime minister Sir Wilfrid Laurier, and is the starting point for city tours. Place du Canada has manicured gardens and was established to honor the nation's dead from both World Wars.

**Place du Canada, Montreal**

# 🔟 Outdoor Activities

**Sightseeing tour boat**

## 1 Boating, Canoeing, and Rafting

**Jetboat excursions: 47 Rue de la Commune Ouest** ■ **(514) 284 9607** ■ **www.jetboatingmontreal.com**

These activities have always been an integral part of life in Montreal. Yachts and sailboats contribute to the colorful marine ambiance of the Vieux-Port in Montreal. Saute-Moutons is the premier Lachine Rapids jetboat (motorized rafting) excursion, departing from the Quai de l'Horloge, while canoeing can be enjoyed on the Canal Lachine.

## 2 Parc Linéaire Le P'tit Train du Nord

**MAP N5**

A former rail track has now been turned into a 144-mile (232-km) hiking, cycling, and cross-country ski trail. The train once took weekenders from Montreal to the part of the Laurentian mountains located at the southern end to Mont-Laurier on the northern extreme.

## 3 Swimming

There are more than 48 indoor pools in the Montreal area, including Olympic-size facilities at Parc Olympique (see pp18–19). In summer there is a beach on Île Notre-Dame, south of Vieux-Port, with a shop, restaurant, and picnic areas.

## 4 Skating and Snowshoeing

Indoor arenas in summer and outdoor city parks and lakes in winter provide numerous ice-skating options in both cities. Snowshoeing is reserved for larger areas such as Parc du Mont-Royal in Montreal.

## 5 Rappelling and Mountain Climbing

**Sépaq: 1-800 665 6527** ■ **www.sepaq.com**

These are two of the fastest growing adventure sports throughout Quebec, with a bevy of challenges available outside both cities. The vast mountainous expanses are overseen by Sépaq (Parks Québec).

## 6 Skiing

Quebec has hundreds of downhill skiing trails throughout the Laurentian, Adirondack, Green, and White Mountain ranges within hours of both cities. The Cantons-de-l'Est (see p87) offer excellent

**Skiing in Les Laurentides**

pistes at Mont Orford, while near Quebec City are ski runs at Mont Sainte-Anne *(see p102)*. Cross-country legends abound in Quebec, with Herman "Jackrabbit" Johannsen at the top of the list. Montreal is filled with large parks ideal for cross-country skiing.

### 7 Dogsledding
**Sépaq: 1-800 665 6527**
Winter dogsled trips are a fantastic way of becoming one with nature as packs of huskies pull you through the forests of the province. Contact Sépaq for more information.

### 8 Biking
Montreal is crisscrossed with bike trails, including along the waterfront, and Quebec City offers unique pedaling paths through historic neighborhoods. The Cantons-de-l'Est boast cycling trails past rolling hills and quiet rivers, with the snow-capped peaks beyond.

**Bicycling in Montreal**

### 9 Horse Riding
**Ranch Mont-Tremblant: (819) 681 4848**
West of Montreal is horse country; make a day of it by touring the rolling hills of Hudson and Rigaud *(see p85)* and be back in the city by nightfall. The Ranch Mont-Tremblant also has a network of trails.

### 10 Ziplining
Aerial forest adventures can be booked at Mont Tremblant, or try an urban zipline circuit over the Old Port of Montreal with MTL Zipline *(see p64)*.

---

**TOP 10 SPECTATOR SPORTS**

**Ice-hockey players in action**

**1 Les Canadiens de Montréal Club de Hockey**
One of the world's most successful professional sports organizations attracts 21,000 fans to the Bell Centre for their famous ice-hockey battles.

**2 Tournoi International de Hockey Pee-Wee de Québec**
The largest youth ice-hockey tournament in the world.

**3 Formula 1 in Montreal**
The planet's fastest drivers tour the Circuit Gilles-Villeneuve in Montreal's annual F1 Grand Prix *(see p56)*.

**4 Québec Capitales Baseball**
Can-Am League's best team plays at the Stade Canac in Quebec City.

**5 Tour de l'Île de Montréal**
The entire city turns out for this bicycle race where cyclists ride over a distance of 62 miles (100 km).

**6 Montréal Alouettes Canadian Football**
Founded in 1946, the Montréal Alouettes play at the Percival Molson Stadium. Their last Grey Cup win was in 2010.

**7 Montreal Impact Soccer**
Montreal's Impact is the city's main soccer team.

**8 Parc Jarry Tennis Championships**
Parc Jarry hosts international professional tennis events.

**9 Grand Prix Cycliste de Montréal**
During this one-day race, cyclists must climb and descend on a 7.5-mile (12-km) circuit that runs around Mont-Royal 17 times.

**10 Montreal Marathon**
Every September hundreds of runners take part in this race through the city.

# Children's Attractions

One of the many hair-raising rides at La Ronde Six Flags Amusement Park

## 1 Centre des Sciences de Montréal

The underlying thrust of this center is to demystify all aspects of science, from technology and how it influences our daily lives, to exploring the underwater world of the ocean. Innovative interactive games make the learning fun. There is an indoor playground for younger kids with a life-size playhouse and large building blocks *(see p64)*.

Centre des Sciences de Montréal

## 2 La Ronde Six Flags Amusement Park, Montreal

MAP F4 ■ 22 chemin Macdonald, Île Ste-Hélène ■ (514) 397 2000 ■ Open May–Oct: daily ■ Adm ■ www.laronde.com

The largest amusement park in Quebec was originally opened for Expo '67. Six Flags took over as owner in 2001 and has added many rides since then. Le Monstre is the world's tallest two-track wooden roller coaster, perfect for thrill-seekers. Tamer rides, such as the family boats rides, mini-trains, and carousels, will appeal to younger children.

## 3 Insectarium, Montreal

4581 Rue Sherbrooke Est ■ Métro Viau, Pie-IX ■ (514) 868 3000 ■ Open daily (times vary) ■ Adm ■ www.espacepourlavie.ca/insectarium

This astounding display celebrates insects of every size and shape. It opened in 1990 thanks to Georges Brossard, who traveled the world to collect the fascinating bugs. Although most of the insects are dead, there are live tarantulas and other creepy crawlies, safely ensconced behind glass *(see p19)*.

## 4 Biodôme, Montreal

4777 Ave Pierre-de-Coubertin ■ Métro Viau ■ (514) 868 3000 ■ Closed for renovations until 2019 ■ Adm ■ www.espacepourlavie.ca/biodome

It is rare to see birds from the northern and southern hemispheres in one place, but in this unusual exhibit, animals from the

Arctic, Antarctic, Tropics, Laurentian, and St Lawrence marine habitats are housed under one roof in controlled settings to resemble their natural habitats *(see p19)*.

### 5 Planétarium Rio Tinto Alcan, Montreal

4801 Ave Pierre-De Coubertin ■ Métro Viau ■ (514) 868 3000 ■ Open 9–5pm Tue–Sun (until 8pm Thu–Sat) ■ Adm ■ www.espacepourlavie.ca/planetarium

Here, visitors are propelled into the heavens courtesy of high-precision technology. A fascinating journey into time and outer space to make sense of the planets and the universe.

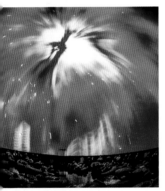

**Planétarium Rio Tinto Alcan**

### 6 Laser Quest, Montreal

MAP G1 ■ 1226 Rue Ste-Catherine Ouest ■ (514) 393 3000 ■ Open daily (hours vary); Mon for private groups only ■ Adm

The dark labyrinth of passageways in this multilevel arena feature fog, specilized lighting, and music. The aim of the game is to find and tag your opponents as often as you can.

### 7 Cosmodôme, Laval

2150 Laurentian Autoroute, Laval ■ (450) 978 3600 ■ Open daily ■ Adm ■ www.cosmodome.org

This museum and education center provides a fascinating look at space and the universe in all its diversity. Large-scale models of the solar system explain the make-up of every planet, while the rockets exhibition provides an insight into space travel.

### 8 Le Théâtre de L'Oeil, Montreal

MAP E1 ■ 7780 Ave Henri-Julien ■ (514) 278 9188 ■ Opening times vary ■ Adm ■ www.theatredeloeil.qc.ca

Performances, workshops, and exhibitions are all part of the fun at this puppet theater. Kids can watch how the puppets are made, learn to pull their strings, and then attend a show.

### 9 Biosphère, Montreal

Housed in Expo '67's iconic American pavilion designed by American architect Buckminster Fuller, the Biosphère is intended to introduce children to environmental issues in an engaging and fun manner *(see p64)*.

**Rocket exhibit, Cosmodôme**

### 10 Zoo do Granby

This well-curated zoo is one of the largest in Canada and features wildlife from all corners of the globe, including zebras from Africa, piranhas and jaguars from South America, and the world's largest felines from Asia. Plus, the zoo abounds with kid-friendly activities like splashing in a wave pool, rafting down the Cunucunoma River, and lively day camps *(see p88)*.

**Elephant at Zoo de Granby**

# TOP 10 Performing Arts Venues

**Auditorium, Théâtre de Quat'Sous**

## 1 Théâtre de Quat'Sous, Montreal

MAP D3 ■ 100 Ave des Pins Est ■ (514) 845 7277 ■ www.quatsous.com

Set in a former synagogue, this brilliant French troupe has given many young performers, writers, and producers their first platform.

## 2 Théâtre d'Aujourd'hui, Montreal

MAP E2 ■ 3900 Rue St-Denis ■ (514) 282 3900 ■ www.theatredaujourdhui.qc.ca

A French theater company founded in 1968, committed to writing, staging, and producing Québécois plays. It is guided by the passion of artistic director Sylvain Bélanger.

## 3 Théâtre du Nouveau Monde, Montreal

MAP K1 ■ 84 Rue Ste-Catherine Ouest ■ (514) 866 8668 ■ www.tnm.qc.ca

Begun in 1951, this is the heart of Québécois theater. The company moved to this heritage building in 1972 and has been putting on legendary shows ever since.

## 4 Place des Arts, Montreal

MAP K1 ■ (514) 842 2112 ■ www.placedesarts.com

The cultural centerpiece of Montreal. Five modern venues and an outdoor plaza house countless performances and are permanent homes to the Orchestre Symphonique de Montréal, Opéra de Montréal, and Les Grands Ballets Canadiens de Montréal. It is also the home of the International Jazz Festival of Montreal, Festival FrancoFolies, and Festival Montréal en Lumière *(see pp56–7)*.

## 5 Grand Théâtre de Québec, Quebec City

MAP H6 ■ 269 Blvd René-Lévesque Est ■ (418) 643 8131 ■ www.grandtheatre.qc.ca

Conceived by Canadian architect and urban theorist Victor Prus, this inventive space uses a stacked concert hall grid to overcome space limitations. Opened in 1971, the theater features a spectacular mural by Quebec artist Jordi Bonet, which leads to the Salle Louis-Fréchette and Octave-Crémazie concert halls. Théâtre du Trident, Opéra de Québec, and the Club Musical de Québec are based here, as well as the Orchestre Symphonique de Québec. Pop concerts are also staged here occasionally.

**Production at Théâtre du Rideau Vert**

## 6 Théâtre du Rideau Vert, Montreal

MAP E2 ■ 4664 Rue St-Denis ■ (514) 844 1793 ■ www.rideauvert.qc.ca

For over 60 years (established in 1949) this French-speaking theater has had an outstanding reputation for the quality of its productions. The program offers everything from classics to contemporary works to international tours.

**Le Capitole de Québec, illuminated during an evening performance**

### 7 Le Capitole de Québec et Cabaret du Capitole, Quebec City

**MAP K5** ▪ **972 Rue St-Jean** ▪ **(418) 694 4444** ▪ **www.lecapitole.com**

Le Capitole is a testament to the committed preservation of historic buildings in Quebec City. Built in 1903 and refurbished by New York architect Thomas W. Lamb in the 1920s, it was given a third lease on life in the 1980s and is now the preferred showcase for theater, cabaret, and cultural events.

### 8 Théâtre du Petit Champlain Maison de la Chanson, Quebec City

**MAP M5** ▪ **68 Rue du Petit Champlain** ▪ **(418) 692 2631** ▪ **www.theatrepetitchamplain.com**

Perhaps the most compelling modern theater in the country is hidden on a crowded stretch of the Rue du Petit Champlain. The building is a beautiful balance of history and contemporary design; inside, the performance space is comfortable and the audience seating generous. The schedule has up-and-coming acts as well as established artists.

### 9 Théâtre de la Bordée, Quebec City

La Bordée has been producing shows since the 1970s and has always been a local favorite. Set in the refurbished Pigalle movie house in the Quartier St-Roch (see p98), this spacious, modern theater features 350 seats. Here, artistic director Michel Nadeau presents contemporary dramas with a touch of political realism. The company has also invited luminaries such as Robert Lepage (see p43) to mount original works.

### 10 Centaur Theatre, Montreal

**MAP K3** ▪ **453 Rue St-François-Xavier** ▪ **(514) 288 3161** ▪ **www.centaur theatre.com**

Montreal's principal English-language theatrical venue was founded in 1969. Housed in the Old Stock Exchange Building, it has two stages and is well-known for its world-class productions. The program varies between Broadway musicals and contemporary Canadian drama, as well as works by international playwrights.

**Entrance to the Centaur Theatre**

# TOP 10 Montreal and Quebec City for Free

**Quebec winter carnival sculpture**

### 1 Free Festivals
The festivals of Montreal and Quebec City feature a huge variety of free shows and performances, from stand-up comedy at Juste pour Rire *(see p56)* to jazz shows at Festival International de Jazz de Montréal *(see p56)* to winter fun at the Carnaval de Québec *(see p57)*.

### 2 Free Days at Museums
There is free admission to the Maison Chevalier *(see p31)* in Quebec City every day, and to the permanent collection at Musée des Beaux-Arts de Montréal *(see pp24–5)*. During UNESCO's International Museum Day (late May), numerous museums are free of charge from 9am until 6pm and provide a free shuttle bus.

**Musée des Beaux-Arts, Montreal**

### 3 Tango Libre

www.tangolibre.ca
It may take two to tango, but in Montreal it also takes no money. The perennially popular Tango Libre offers free introductory classes, at various parks in the summer and in studios in the winter.

### 4 Maisons de la Culture

www.accesculture.com
Montreal's secret for free entertainment is the Maisons de la Culture network, which is a series of venues offering complimentary performances, from performing arts to photography, by local artists.

### 5 Church Concerts
www.montrealcathedral.ca, www.notre-dame-de-quebec.org
Numerous churches and cathedrals host free concerts, including the Christ Church Cathedral in Montreal and the Basilique-Cathédrale Notre-Dame-de-Québec in Quebec City. Also, you can celebrate Sunday mass at 11am at Montreal's Notre-Dame Basilica *(see pp16–17)* to the uplifting sounds of a choir.

### 6 City Parks
Montreal's Parc du Mont-Royal *(see pp12–13)*, which elegantly presides over the city, abounds with free outdoor activities, from strolling the shaded paths to floating toy boats at Lac Aux Castor (Beaver Lake). Just northeast of Quebec City, explore the lush greenery and trickling streams of Parc Chauveau.

### 7 McGill University

Stroll through a Neo-Classical stone gate to enter McGill, Montreal's prestigious university, which is filled with free arts and culture. The Musée Redpath showcases a top-notch natural history collection and the campus is dotted with sculptures, notably Raymond Mason's *The Illuminated Crowd*. You can often catch free performances at the Schulich School of Music *(see p70)*.

**Musée Redpath, McGill University**

### 8 Free Walking Tours

www.freemontrealtours.com,
www.afreetourofquebec.com

Explore both cities on free walking tours, like the Free Old Montreal Tour, a historical and cultural tour led by a local, and A Free Tour of Quebec.

### 9 Art Mûr Gallery, Montreal

5826 rue St-Hubert ▪ (514) 933 0711 ▪ Closed Sun–Mon ▪ www.artmur.com

Peruse contemporary art by award-winning artists from around Canada, and the world, at this free gallery.

### 10 Théâtre de Verdure

www.accesculture.com/
contenu/theatredeverdure

This amphitheater, located in Montreal's Parc de la Fontaine, features a diverse array of free performances in summer that includes theater, dance, and music.

**TOP 10 BUDGET TIPS**

**1** Wednesday evenings admission is free at the McCord Museum *(see p69)* and half-price at the MAC *(see p70)*.

**2** Quebec City and Montreal are famous for cheap comfort food outlets, including *casse-croûtes* (snack bars).

**3** *Friperies* (secondhand clothiers) sell fashions from every era and style at cheap prices. Rue St-Denis, Avenue Mont-Royal, Rue Ste-Catherine Est, and Boulevard St-Laurent in Montreal are good places to scout.

**4** Sleep for cheap at youth hostels, including Samesun Montréal and the HI Quebec City.

**5** Pick up the Passeport MTL card (www.passeportmtl.com), which offers free access to key city attractions and unlimited use of public transport.

**6** Nab same-day discount tickets to the symphony, opera, theater, comedy, and more through La Vitrine (www.lavitrine.com), a ticket booth at Montreal's Place des Arts in downtown.

**7** For a cheap night out, head to *apportez votre vin* ("bring your own wine") restaurants. Before dinner, enjoy the *cinq à sept* (5–7pm happy hour).

**8** The Express Bus 747 (www.stm.info) is the cheapest ride between the airport and Montreal's city center.

**9** Check the local papers for free or discounted entertainment; the Vieux-Port areas in both Montreal and Quebec City regularly present outdoor concerts and firework displays for free.

**10** Munch on wedges of Québécois cheese, olives, warm bread rolls, and other complimentary local samples at Jean-Talon Market and Atwater Market in Montreal, and Le Marché du Vieux-Port in Quebec City.

**Apples on sale, Jean-Talon Market**

**Festivals and Events**

### 1 Carnaval de Québec

Late Jan–Feb ■ www.carnaval.qc.ca

Few events define Quebec City like the Carnaval de Québec, one of the largest winter festivals in the world. Among the festival highlights are the fairytale Palais de Glace (Ice Palace), which is constructed from 6,000 frozen blocks of ice; the International Snow Sculpture competition; parades; and Québécois food and drink, including Caribou, made with vodka, sherry, port, brandy, and maple sugar.

**Bonhomme, the Carnaval mascot**

### 2 Festival Montréal en Lumière

www.montrealenlumiere.com

The spirits of Montrealers are given a boost during the winter months in this celebration of life through light. Each night over the festival's two-week run in February, organizers host a wild combination of attractions, from outdoor sound and light (son et lumière) productions, to indoor concerts, illuminated buildings, theater and dance performances, culinary soirées of traditional foods, and nightly fireworks. This is a spectacular time to be visiting the city.

### 3 Les FrancoFolies de Montréal

Jun ■ www.francofolies.com

A wildly eclectic music festival celebrating all types of French music. Over 500,000 people attend concerts by groups far from the mainstream of North American culture, with styles ranging from hip-hop to creole, rap, swing and, of course, traditional French songs.

### 4 Grand Prix du Canada

www.gpcanada.ca

Montreal hosts the world's fastest drivers each year for its Formula 1 Grand Prix, drawing thousands of visitors from across the globe. The event is held at the Circuit Gilles-Villeneuve, named after the French-Canadian racing driver.

### 5 Festival d'Été de Québec

www.infofestival.com

For ten exciting days each July, Quebec City becomes one mammoth outdoor music stage as performers flock from all over the world to perform countless styles of music. This enormous spectacle is the most spirited activity of the summer, with 500 shows and some 1,000 artists blasting out their sounds at over 15 different performance venues.

**The Strumbellas perform live at the Festival d'Été de Québec**

### 6 Just For Laughs Festival
www.hahaha.com

Over 1.5 million jolly patrons attend a banquet of mirth each year in July at Montreal's comedy festival (Juste pour Rire). From quirky free shows staged in the Quartier Latin streets to the constantly sold-out Club Series and Loto-Québec Galas, humor in all its forms is on offer from more than 600 international performers.

### 7 Le Festival International de Jazz de Montréal
Late Jun–Jul ■ www.montreal jazzfest.com

The world's largest jazz festival takes over the concourse at Place des Arts in downtown Montreal, as well as neighborhood clubs, restaurants, and parks. Each year several million visitors party for 11 days of free outdoor concerts and a wide variety of musical events involving internationally renowned musicians.

**L'International des Feux Loto-Québec**

### 8 L'International des Feux Loto-Québec
Wed & Sat: 10pm ■ www.laronde.com

From early July to early August the skies over Vieux-Montréal light up twice a week with explosive theatrics for the Montreal Fireworks Festival, held at La Ronde amusement park (see pp50–51). Countries from around the world participate in this display of pyrotechnic talents, which is recognized as one of the most prestigious in the world. The beautiful fireworks are best viewed from the stands at La Ronde.

**Fêtes de la Nouvelle-France**

### 9 Fêtes de la Nouvelle-France
www.nouvellefrance.qc.ca

A large-scale voyage back in time transforms Place Royale and the Basse-Ville section of Quebec City into a magical melange of period costumes, traditional music and dance, and authentic foods, all to celebrate the settling of the city by the French in the 1600s (see p40). Early August crowds are invited to attend over 600 performances by local actors, musicians, dancers, and artists.

### 10 Rendez-vous ès TRAD
www.cvpv.net

A superb multicultural festival each fall at Chapelle du Musée de l'Amérique Francophone in Vieux-Québec (see p30) offers a sensuous feast of traditional music, dance, crafts, foods, and laughter. Share homespun hilarity while watching teams joust during *joute chantée* (an improvised singing tournament), or during the culinary fun of *souper chanté* (singing supper). Singers come from as far afield as Guatemala, Japan, Greece, Martinique, and Senegal.

# Montreal and Quebec City Area by Area

Colorful Mont Tremblant Village
in Les Laurentides during fall

# TOP 10 Vieux-Montréal and Vieux-Port

This enchanting area, established in 1642, is a rewarding spot to begin a tour of the city of Montreal. Its ancient churches, cobblestone streets, horse-drawn *calèches*, and the bustling international port characterize this fascinating neighborhood. Vieux-Montréal epitomizes the romance, culture, and *joie-de-vivre* of the metropolis, while the activity of mega-freighters and cruise boats in the Vieux-Port reveals that Montreal is the shipping gateway to the Great Lakes. The old quarter combines high-tech novelty with old-world charm as well as some of the city's best dining options. Plan to spend several days exploring the craft shops, museums, cultural exhibitions, and French bistros while savoring the European-style yet informal Québécois hospitality.

**Statue atop Notre-Dame-de-Bon-Secours**

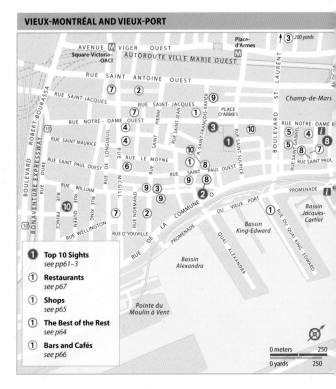

**VIEUX-MONTRÉAL AND VIEUX-PORT**

1 **Top 10 Sights**
see pp61–3

1 **Restaurants**
see p67

1 **Shops**
see p65

1 **The Best of the Rest**
see p64

1 **Bars and Cafés**
see p66

0 meters   250
0 yards    250

**Basilique Notre-Dame altar**

### 1 Basilique Notre-Dame

When the largest bell in North America begins to thunder over Place d'Armes, legions of pigeons create a spectacle reminiscent of St Peter's Square in Rome. Meanwhile throngs of pilgrims and visitors flock daily to this compelling architectural masterpiece (see pp16–17).

### 2 Musée Pointe-à-Callière

This striking modern building, married with the ancient Place Royale setting, vibrates with activity throughout the year, as visitors digest one cultural exhibition treat after another on display inside and outside this museum (see pp22–3).

### 3 Séminaire St-Sulpice

MAP K3 ▪ 116 Rue Notre-Dame Ouest ▪ (514) 849 6561

Erected between 1685 and 1687 for the Sulpician religious order, the St Sulpice Seminary is the second oldest surviving building in Montreal. This remarkable historic edifice remains an icon of the institutional architecture that was employed in Nouvelle-France. The Sulpicians' clock above the main doorway is one of the oldest of its kind in North America, dating from 1701 (see p17). Closed to the public, the Seminary occasionally offers tours in the summer.

**Montreal's Hôtel de Ville**

### 4 Hôtel de Ville

MAP L2 ▪ 275 Rue Notre-Dame Est ▪ Open 8am–5pm Mon–Fri

The town hall was a gracious Second Empire-style edifice built between 1872 and 1878 by architect Henri-Maurice Perrault (1828–1903). Damaged by fire in 1922, it was rebuilt a year later in Beaux-Arts style, and is still used for its original function. You can visit the interior and free guided tours are offered in the summer. It is best seen at night when it illuminates the sky (see p45).

View of Marché Bonsecours from across the Bassin Bonsecours

### 5 Marché Bonsecours

MAP L3 ■ 350 Rue St-Paul Est ■ Open 10am–6pm daily (to 9pm Jun–Sep; other late shopping evenings vary according to season)

This greystone Neo-Classical building has a rich history. It once housed the Parliament of Canada and was even a theatrical venue for Charles Dickens when he acted at the Théâtre Royal in 1842. Today it is a shopping center that attracts a continuing influx of visitors under its shining dome (see p44).

### 6 Place Jacques-Cartier and Place de la Dauversière

MAP L3

Two famous names in Canadian history have beautiful squares across from each other. Place Jacques-Cartier (see p45) celebrates the discoverer of Canada (see p40), while Place de la Dauversière honors Jerome le Royer, Sieur de la Dauversière of La Flèche in Anjou, France, the Royal Tax Collector whose idea it was to build a colony here, eventually called Ville-Marie.

### 7 Musée Marguerite-Bourgeoys and Chapelle Notre-Dame-de-Bon-Secours

MAP L3 ■ 400 Rue St-Paul Est ■ (514) 282 8670 ■ Open Tue–Sun (opening times vary) ■ Adm ■ www.margueritebourgeoys.org

In 1653 Marguerite Bourgeoys arrived in Ville-Marie to open a school, which began in a stable assigned to her by the Sieur de Maisonneuve. By 1655 she was head of the Congregation of the Sisters of Notre-Dame and oversaw the construction of Canada's first stone church in 1675. The chapel that remains dates from 1771. It is known as the "Sailors Chapel," given its portside location and model ships hanging throughout.

### 8 Musée Château Ramezay

MAP L3 ■ 280 Rue Notre-Dame Est ■ (514) 861 3708 ■ Open Jun–Oct: 9:30am–6pm daily; Nov–May: 10am–4:30pm Tue–Sun ■ Adm ■ www.chateauramezay.qc.ca

This elegant stone home was constructed to house the Governor of Montreal, Claude de Ramezay (1659–1724), and his 16 children. It was thereafter known as the Maison des Castors (beavers) because it was home to the Compagnie des Indes (West Indies Company) and their burgeoning fur trade with Europe.

**THE FRENCH ARRIVAL AND THE FUR TRADE**

The original Huron village of Hochelaga (meaning "where the rivers meet") provided the French explorers with an ideal location from which to settle the new continent and the key staging area for exploration of the rest of North America. It also allowed access to the Huron fur-trading networks, resulting in an enormously profitable fur trade between Canada and Europe.

In 1775 General Richard Montgomery lived here with his band of rebellious Americans while they made a failed attempt to capture the city for the US. It has been a museum since 1895, illustrating the early settlement of Quebec, from tools to uniforms to historic documents. Of note is the Nantes Salon, lavishly decorated by 18th-century French architect, Germain Boffrand (see p44).

### 9 Sir George-Étienne-Cartier National Historic Site

**MAP L3** ▪ 458 Rue Notre-Dame Est ▪ (514) 283 2282 ▪ Open Jun–Dec (opening times vary) ▪ Adm ▪ pc.gc.ca

Preserved artifacts of the 19th-century upper-middle classes and their lifestyle are exhibited at Sir George-Étienne-Cartier's house. Cartier was one of the Fathers of Canadian Confederation and his home, where he lived from 1848 to 1871, provides an insight into the mores of his social class at that time (see p45).

**Sir George-Étienne-Cartier's home**

### 10 Darling Foundry

**MAP J3** ▪ 745 Ottawa St ▪ (514) 392 1554 ▪ Open noon–7pm Wed–Sun (to 10pm Thu) ▪ Adm ▪ www.fonderiedarling.org

This art space, which is housed in a converted foundry building, is home to changing exhibitions by visiting artists, with a focus on contemporary art. The Foundry also hosts openings and readings. It is the center of an expanding creative network, the Quartier Ephémère, in this former industrial district. Free on Thursdays.

## AN AFTERNOON STROLL ALONG THE WATERFRONT

### ▶ AFTERNOON

Start your walk with a visit to the **Darling Foundry**, a cavernous contemporary art space at the western edge of Vieux-Montréal. Located on a small street in a warren of former industrial buildings, it contains some impressive works from Quebec and international artists that are worth the detour. Afterwards, walk over to Rue McGill and pop into the sleek and chic resto-boutique **Le Cartet** at No. 106 for a delicious lunch that can be eaten on-site or taken with you. Their coffee is fantastic, too.

Next, head east along the waterfront where you may find secondhand booksellers, yachts of the rich and famous, and portrait artists vying for your attention. Stay beside the water, past the **Centre des Sciences de Montréal** (see p64) to **Bassin Bonsecours**, the waterfall, and **Quai de l'Horloge** (see p64).

Go north to the **Chapelle Notre-Dame-de-Bon-Secours** (400 Rue St-Paul Est) where, if you are feeling energetic, you can climb the interior stairs for a wonderful view of the Vieux-Port, then go directly across the street to **Auberge Pierre du Calvet** (see p64). Take a peek inside at the sumptuous period surroundings.

End your walk by strolling through **Marché Bonsecours**, with its designer boutiques, then continue along Rue St-Paul and start the evening with a cocktail on the **Hôtel Nelligan**'s rooftop, which has breathtaking views (see p114).

*See map on pp60–61* ←

# The Best of the Rest

**1 Centre des Sciences de Montréal**

MAP K3 ▪ Quai King-Edward ▪ (514) 496 4724 ▪ Open 9am–4pm Mon–Fri, 10am–5pm Sat & Sun ▪ Adm ▪ www.centredessciences demontreal.com

This science and technology center offers quality entertainment for kids (and adults) with its games, IMAX theater, and interactive exhibits *(see p50)*.

**2 Auberge Pierre du Calvet**

MAP L3 ▪ 405 Rue Bonsecours ▪ (514) 282 1725 ▪ www.pierreducalvet.ca

One of the most romantic spots in Montreal, this 1725 inn presents an outstanding collection of antiques. Dine in Les Filles du Roy restaurant for some delectable cuisine.

**3 Centre d'Histoire de Montréal**

MAP K3 ▪ 335 Place d'Youville ▪ (514) 872 3207 ▪ Open 10am–5pm Wed–Sun ▪ Adm

This former firehall has an interactive exhibition with local treasures.

**Exhibit, Centre d'Histoire de Montréal**

**4 Quai de l'Horloge**

MAP M3

Climb the interior stairs of this 1922 clock tower for views over the port.

**5 MTL Zipline**

MAP L3 ▪ Hangar 16, 363 Rue de la Commune Est ▪ (514) 947 5463 ▪ Open May–Oct: 10am–10pm daily

This urban zipline circuit offers visitors a bird's-eye view of the city, beginning at the Vieux-Port.

**Biosphère at Parc Jean-Drapeau**

**6 Biosphère**

MAP F5 ▪ 160 chemin Tour-de-l'Isle, Ile Ste-Hélène ▪ (514) 283 5000 ▪ Opening times vary, call ahead to check ▪ Adm

An architectural centerpiece created for Expo '67, the dome now acts as an Ecowatch Centre and a museum dedicated to the St Lawrence River and Great Lakes *(see p51)*.

**7 Square Victoria**

MAP J2

In 1860 a magnificent monument to honor Queen Victoria was erected on this haymarket square.

**8 Old Customs House**

This archetypal example of 1830s Neo-Classical architecture is today incorporated into the Musée Pointe-à-Callière *(see p23)*.

**9 Bank of Montreal Museum**

MAP K2 ▪ 129 Rue St-Jacques Ouest ▪ Open 10am–4pm Mon–Fri

The oldest bank in Canada (1817) houses an interesting currency museum within an ornate interior.

**10 Stewart Museum at the Fort**

MAP F4 ▪ 20 chemin Tour-de-l'Isle, Ile Ste-Hélène ▪ Open 10am–5pm Wed–Sun (Jul & Aug Tue–Sun) ▪ Adm

Montreal's only fort reveals over 400 years of military history.

# Shops

### 1 Marché Bonsecours
A Vieux-Montréal heritage landmark is now a bustling area of designer boutiques *(see p62)*.

### 2 Centre de Commerce Mondial
MAP J2 ■ 747 Rue du Square-Victoria

An inspiring architectural concept has been created by interlinking Ruelle des Fortifications heritage structures under a spectacular glass atrium. Shops, restaurants, offices, and a hotel can all be found here.

### 3 Galerie Michel-Ange
MAP L3 ■ 430 Rue Bonsecours

A reliable art gallery featuring many fine Québécois and international painters, which is located in a heritage house built in 1864.

### 4 Galerie le Chariot
MAP L3 ■ 446 Place Jacques-Cartier

A wonderful Inuit art collection awaits souvenir hunters in this gallery on Place Jacques-Cartier. One of the first businesses to preserve buildings in the Old Town, Galerie Le Chariot has treasures that will suit all budgets.

### 5 Camtec Photo
MAP K3 ■ 26 Rue Notre-Dame Est

Probably one of the last camera shops in the city, this is the place for all your photography needs. Vintage equipment as well as brand new gear can be found here. They even have their own laboratory on the premises.

### 6 Conseil des Métiers d'Art du Québec
MAP L3 ■ 350 Rue St-Paul Est

A sensational cooperative featuring Québécois artists working with varied materials. Choose from paintings, prints, and jewelry to clothing, toys, cards, glasswork, marionettes, and other fabulous gifts.

### 7 Le Cartet Boutique Alimentaire
MAP J3 ■ 106 Rue McGill

Drop in at this culinary emporium for the most delicious treats and foodstuffs. With goodies from around the planet, this tempting shop will set your senses ablaze.

### 8 Denis Gagnon
MAP K3 ■ 170B Rue St-Paul Ouest

This *enfant terrible* of the Quebec fashion scene has been wowing international audiences for years with his original and daring designs.

### 9 Espace Pepin
MAP J3 ■ 350 Rue St-Paul Ouest

With a natural vibe, this art concept store offers locally and ethically designed clothing and home decor.

### 10 Noël Eternel
MAP K3 ■ 60 Rue Notre-Dame Ouest

A store dedicated to the idea of keeping the Christmas spirit alive throughout the year. Stock up on unusual hand-crafted adornments, wrapping paper, stockings, games, dolls, and lots more.

**Noël Eternel's sparkling display**

*See map on pp60–61*

# Bars and Cafés

### 1 L'Assommoir Notre-Dame
MAP K3 ■ 211 Rue Notre-Dame Ouest ■ www.assommoir.com

A chic place to grab a drink and a light meal, this bar is a mixologist's delight. It boasts over 250 cocktails, including 50 different martinis, an impressive beer selection, and an extensive wine cellar.

Cocktails at La Champagnerie

### 2 La Champagnerie
MAP L3 ■ 343 Rue St-Paul Est ■ www.lachampagnerie.ca

Toast the night at this buzzy bar that celebrates bubbly in all its glory, from French Champagne to Spanish cava. Enjoy creative cocktails and tasty nibbles, like duck carpaccio with fig.

### 3 Le Mal Nécessaire
MAP K2 ■ 1106 B Blvd St-Laurent ■ www.lemalnecessaire.com

For Polynesian cocktails and delicious Chinese fusion, try this stylish tiki bar in Chinatown.

### 4 Santos
MAP L3 ■ 191 Rue St-Paul Est ■ www.ilovesantos.ca

For a relaxed evening in Vieux-Montréal, head to laid-back Santos, where you can sample unusual tapas-style foods. Listen to live jazz during the week, and DJs play on weekends.

### 5 L'Auberge Saint-Gabriel
MAP K3 ■ 426 Rue St-Gabriel ■ www.aubergesaint-gabriel.com

One of the oldest inns in North America (1688) is now a bar-restaurant set in a romantic location. The popular Velvet bar offers an extensive wine selection.

### 6 Auberge Pierre du Calvet
MAP L3 ■ 405 Rue Bonsecours ■ www.pierreducalvet.ca

A celebrated inn where Benjamin Franklin met with the Sons of Liberty in 1775. It has a cozy lounge with a fireplace and atrium garden where breakfast is served *(see p64)*.

### 7 Bevo
MAP L3 ■ 410 Rue St-Vincent ■ www.bevopizza.com

Tucked away in a historic building on a tiny street, this bar serves traditional wood-fired pizzas while DJs spin on the weekends.

### 8 Pub BreWskey
MAP L3 ■ 380 Rue St-Paul Est ■ www.brewskey.ca

This pub brews its own craft beers, plus serves whiskies and cocktails. The kitchen stays open until 3am and the patio is perfect for warm days.

### 9 Stash Café
MAP K3 ■ 200 Rue St-Paul Ouest ■ www.restaurantstashcafe.ca

A favorite actors' hangout near the Centaur Theatre *(see p53)*, this Polish café-restaurant has a superb kitchen serving hearty *borscht* soup, with live piano music in the evenings.

### 10 Tapas 24
MAP J3 ■ 420 Rue Notre-Dame Ouest ■ www.tapas24.ca

Spirited restaurant serving Spanish tapas with a Québécois twist, such as cod croquettes with maple syrup.

Sleek interior at Tapas 24

# Restaurants

**PRICE CATEGORIES**
For a three-course meal for one with half a bottle of wine (or equivalent meal), taxes and extra charges.
.................................................
$ under $40 ■ $$ $40–$80 ■ $$$ over $80

**1 Garde Manger**
MAP K3 ■ 408 Rue St-François-Xavier ■ (514) 678 5044 ■ www. garde manger.ca ■ $$$

This upscale seafood eatery is owned by the Montreal celebrity chef Chuck Hughes. Try the lobster risotto or, for the more gluttonous, the famed lobster *poutine (see p111).*

**2 Olive & Gourmando**
MAP J3 ■ 351 Rue St-Paul Est ■ (514) 350 1083 ■ www.oliveet gourmando.com ■ $

Delightful and rustic, this bakery is known for its brunch. It also serves pastries, grilled paninis, and salads.

**3 Restaurant Chez L'Epicier**
MAP L3 ■ 311 Rue St-Paul Est ■ (514) 878 2232 ■ www.chezlepicier. com ■ $$$

A fabulous grocery store, sit-down restaurant, and take-out service, all under one roof. Inventive soups, salads, and locally produced cheeses, meats, and herbs can be found here.

**4 Boris Bistro**
MAP J3 ■ 465 Rue McGill ■ (514) 848 9575 ■ www.boris bistro.com ■ $$

A sensational mix is on the menu here – sit in the lush garden and try French fries cooked in duck fat or divine poached salmon.

**5 Club Chasse et Pêche**
MAP L3 ■ 423 Rue St-Claude ■ (514) 861 1112 ■ www.leclub chasseetpeche.com ■ $$$

This high-end restaurant, housed in an attractive low, red-brick building, serves a robust mix of fresh seafood and hearty meat dishes in an intimate dining space.

**Sophisticated dining at Holder**

**6 Holder**
MAP J3 ■ 407 Rue McGill ■ (514) 849 0333 ■ www. restaurantholder.com ■ $$

This elegant Holder brothers restaurant-brasserie exudes flair and good taste.

**7 Marusan Comptoir Japonais**
MAP J3 ■ 401 Notre-Dame Ouest ■ (514) 289 1115 ■ www.marusan.ca ■ $

Compact and modern space with authentic Japanese izakaya classics. Thursday's happy hour includes a DJ.

**8 Restaurant Solmar**
MAP L3 ■ 111 Rue St-Paul Est ■ (514) 861 4562 ■ www.solmar-montreal.com ■ $$

A Portuguese mainstay renowned for its lobster, steaks, and squid.

**9 Gibby's**
MAP K3 ■ 298 Place d'Youville ■ (514) 282 1837 ■ www.gibbys.com ■ $$$

One of Canada's finest eateries, with a courtyard garden and a menu that's big on oysters and steak.

**10 Le 400 Coups**
MAP J3 ■ 400 Rue Notre-Dame Est ■ (514) 985 0400 ■ www.les400coups.ca ■ $$$

An elegant Vieux-Montréal mainstay, this restaurant serves traditional French cuisine with a modern twist.

*See map on pp60–61*

# TOP 10 Downtown and Quartier Latin

The two most animated and colorful areas of central Montreal offer a cornucopia of delights. Though tiny by many mega-city standards, these *quartiers* (districts) are intriguing components of Montreal's urban landscape, bustling with activity around the clock. They are home to many artists, designers, musicians, writers, and academics, as well as students from both Concordia and McGill universities, all of whom are attracted by the eclectic mélange of historic sights, wonderful museums, LGBT+ venues, multi-ethnic restaurants and enclaves, colorful bars, and entrepreneurial businesses. Day-trippers, sightseers, and suburban residents contribute equally to this vigorous canvas. No visit to Montreal would be complete without spending at least a couple of days exploring these two magnetic areas of the city.

**Figure, Musée Redpath**

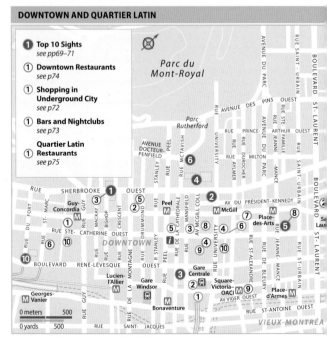

**DOWNTOWN AND QUARTIER LATIN**

1 Top 10 Sights
see pp69–71

1 Downtown Restaurants
see p74

1 Shopping in Underground City
see p72

1 Bars and Nightclubs
see p73

Quartier Latin
1 Restaurants
see p75

**Musée des Beaux-Arts**

### 1 Musée des Beaux-Arts

One of the oldest Canadian bastions of visual and decorative arts. The museum houses vast permanent collections and visiting exhibitions heralding the accomplishments of contemporary artists, as well as creative works by masters from other eras *(see pp24–5)*.

### 2 McCord Museum of Canadian History

MAP J1 ■ 690 Rue Sherbrooke Ouest ■ (514) 861 6701 ■ Open 10am–6pm Tue–Fri (to 9pm Wed), 10am–5pm Sat & Sun ■ Adm ■ www.musee-mccord.qc.ca

The single most important First Nations (native Canadian) collection of artifacts in Quebec is on display at the McCord Museum, and includes the most extensive library of costumes and textiles in Canada. A particularly thrilling attraction is the Notman Photographic Archives, which records life in Montreal, Quebec, and Canada from 1840 to 1935. Over one million pictures are preserved and identified in more than 200 albums, which experts around the world use for research.

### 3 Cathédrale Marie-Reine-du-Monde

MAP H2 ■ 1085 Rue de la Cathédrale ■ Open 7am–6pm Mon–Fri, 7:30am–6pm Sat & Sun

Reminiscent of Saint Peter's Basilica in Rome, the cathedral was built in the 19th century to service the local Catholic community. It continues to attract visitors and residents, not least because of outstanding architectural features such as the Neo-Baroque copper and gold baldachin above the altarpiece. This church remains firmly at the heart of Montreal's downtown activity.

**Cathédrale Marie-Reine-du-Monde**

**THE HEART OF FRENCH NATIONALISM**

The Quartier Latin neighborhood, thought by some to be the center of French nationalism in Quebec, remains a bastion of independent thinkers, artists, writers, academics, and students, who contribute to a lively backdrop for the ongoing intellectual and political debate concerning the French role in Canada.

Exhibition hall, Musée Redpath

### 4 McGill University
MAP J1 ■ 845 Rue Sherbrooke Ouest

The campus spreads out over 80 lush acres (32 ha) of the downtown district. The land was a bequest from Scottish fur-trader James McGill in 1821 and was chartered by King George IV. Fine examples of Victorian architecture mix easily with the contemporary bustle of student life, making the 300 buildings on campus a testament to McGill's personal dream and a city's passion for education – McGill's School of Medicine is one of the finest.

### 5 Musée d'Art Contemporain de Montréal
MAP K1 ■ 185 Rue Ste-Catherine Ouest ■ (514) 847 6226 ■ Open 11am–6pm Tue–Sun (until 9pm Wed) ■ Adm ■ www.macm.org

Dedicated solely to contemporary art, this high-profile institution has an innovative program of exhibitions highlighting the work of artists from Canada and the international circuit.

### 6 Musée Redpath
MAP C3 ■ 859 Rue Sherbrooke Ouest ■ Open 9am–5pm Mon–Fri, 11am–5pm Sun ■ www.mcgill.ca/redpath

The museum was opened in 1882 to house the collections of Sir William Dawson, a noted Canadian natural scientist. Part of McGill's Faculty of Science, it now displays biological, geological, and cultural artifacts. The building is also notable – built in 1880, it is steeped in Victorian Classicism and Greek Revival architecture.

### 7 Chinatown
MAP L2

Canada's transcontinental railway system owes a great debt to the many Chinese laborers who made it a reality. After 1880, when the railway was finished, Chinese workers decided to settle in Montreal and gathered together in this enclave to protect themselves against local discrimination. Today the area is also home to many other Southeast Asian communities. A stroll through the lantern-lit streets around Boulevard

The large campus of the Musée d'Art Contemporain de Montréal

Saint-Laurent and Rue de la Gauchetière reveals bargain boutiques and inexpensive ethnic eateries.

### (8) Chapelle Notre-Dame-de-Lourdes

MAP L1 ■ 430 Rue Ste-Catherine Est ■ (514) 845 8278 ■ Open 11am–6pm Mon–Fri, 10:30am–6:30pm Sat, 9am–6:30pm Sun ■ www.cndlm.org

This richly decorated chapel, erected in 1876 for the Sulpician Order, is the greatest achievement of artist Napoleon Bourassa, grandson of Louis-Joseph Papineau, leader of the reformist Patriote movement. Bourassa studied in Paris, Rome, and Venice, returning to Montreal with the desire to create fine art as an expression of patriotism and faith.

### (9) Gay Village

MAP M1

Montreal is a gay-friendly city, and one of the most festive parades belongs to this community. Between Rue St-Hubert and Avenue Papineau, the Village is alive around the clock. Restored homes mix with contemporary condominiums to create a diverse and exciting area.

**Rue Ste-Catherine Est in Gay Village**

### (10) Canadian Centre for Architecture

MAP B4 ■ 1920 Rue Baile ■ (514) 939 7026 ■ Open 11am–6pm Wed–Sun (until 9pm Thu) ■ Adm (except Thu evenings) ■ www.cca.qc.ca

Opened in 1979 to build public awareness about architecture, the center promotes scholarly research in the field and stimulates innovation in design practice. Its collections include models, drawings, and photographs of some of the world's most important buildings.

---

**AN AFTERNOON WALK THROUGH CHINATOWN AND QUARTIER LATIN**

▶ **AFTERNOON**

Start at **St Patrick's Basilica** *(corner of Rue St-Alexandre and Blvd René-Lévesque Ouest)* to explore the nave of this wonderful church, then take Rue de la Gauchetière east across to **Avenue Viger Ouest**. Notice the beautiful Chinese lantern streetlights while you continue on to the bargain shops, *dim sum* restaurants, fresh produce markets, and herbal stores.

Head to **Boulevard St-Laurent**, the lively heart of Chinatown and the main street dividing Montreal into east and west. Stop at the corner of Boulevard St-Laurent and **Boulevard Renée-Lévesque** and gaze up at a huge mural that marks one of the entrances to Chinatown. Stroll to **Le Mal Nécessaire** *(see p66)*, a subterranean tiki bar, for Hawaii-inspired drinks.

Make your way to **Rue St-Denis** and turn left. You now get to savor the effervescence of the Quartier-Latin, with its boutiques, restaurants, bistros, and cafés. Pop into any one of the strip's small shops, or rest and have a drink or snack on the huge front and back terraces of **Bar Le Saint-Sulpice** *(see p73)*. Continue north to **Carré St-Louis**, the center of the quarter, with a distinctly French ambiance. Beautiful *belle époque* homes abound in this area, especially on **Avenue Laval**.

Continue the French theme for dinner on the terrace of **Café Cherrier** *(see p75)*.

---

*See map on pp68–9* ←

# Shopping in Underground City

### 1 Le 1000
MAP J2 ▪ 1000 Rue de la Gauchetière Ouest

Inside Montreal's tallest building, under a glass dome, visitors will find an indoor skating rink surrounded by shops, fast food counters, and a gym.

### 2 Place Alexis Nihon
1500 Rue Atwater

With a good-value food court, plus direct access to the metro, this shopping mall has it all. The variety of stores here include a pharmacy, multiple big brand clothing stores and a department store.

### 3 Place Montréal Trust
MAP J1 ▪ 1500 Ave McGill College

Place Montréal Trust boasts the highest spouting water fountain in North America at 100 ft (30 m), exclusive fashion outlets, and a large food court.

### 4 Promenades Cathédrale
MAP J1 ▪ 625 Rue Ste-Catherine Ouest

This remarkable underground shopping concourse, consisting of 60 stores and restaurants, is built beneath the Christ Church Cathedral (1859).

### 5 Les Cours Mont-Royal
MAP H1 ▪ 1455 Rue Peel

At the western end of the central shopping network, this attractive mall has the distinction of being set in the 1920s Mont-Royal Hotel, presenting elegant shops over four levels above and below ground.

### 6 La Baie
MAP J1 ▪ 585 Rue Ste-Catherine Ouest

Also known as Hudson's Bay Company and The Bay in the rest of the country, this is a historic Canadian department store. You will find all the standard fare here, from fashion and accessories to household goods.

### 7 Complexe Desjardins
MAP K1 ▪ 150 Rue Ste-Catherine Ouest

Standing across from the Place des Arts, this predominantly French mall is connected to Complex Guy-Favreau and Chinatown via underground tunnels.

**Centre Eaton shopping mall**

### 8 Centre Eaton
MAP J1 ▪ Rue Ste-Catherine Ouest

A light-filled glass cavern forms the entrance to this multilayered shopping and dining mall. The center also stages fashion and art events.

### 9 Place Ville-Marie
MAP J1 ▪ 1 Place Ville-Marie

Place Ville-Marie attracts consumers in large numbers, but an additional bonus is its tranquil, leafy outdoor square – a summer lunchtime oasis.

### 10 Faubourg Sainte-Catherine
MAP G1 ▪ 1616 Rue Ste-Catherine Ouest

Located in the heart of Shaughnessy Village this colorful glass mall is known for its fresh market produce and inexpensive eateries.

# Bars and Nightclubs

**1 Club Stéréo**
MAP M1 ■ 858 Rue Ste-Catherine Est

One of the most powerful audio systems in any club in North America continues to pack this after-hours dance floor. A cross section of music styles attracts party animals.

**2 Bar Cloakroom**
MAP J1 ■ 2175 Rue de la Montagne

A cozy, kind-of-hidden, bespoke speakeasy that has no official menu. Let the master mixologists make you what you want.

**3 Pub l'Île Noir**
MAP L1 ■ 1649 Rue St-Denis

An authentic Scottish pub with wood decor and an excellent selection of single malt scotches and imported draught beer. The summer patio is great for people-watching.

**4 Complexe Sky**
MAP M1 ■ 1478 Rue Ste-Catherine Est

This amazingly large complex features a pub, a dance club, and a cabaret to entertain the large and growing LBGT+ community on the east side of downtown.

Outdoor seating, Les 3 Brasseurs

**5 Les 3 Brasseurs**
MAP L1 ■ 1658 Rue St-Denis

A lively location that opens onto Rue St-Denis on two sides with a superb terrace overlooking the flow of festivities. Serves wholesome cuisine and home-brewed beer.

Drinks being poured at La Distillerie No. 1

**6 La Distillerie No. 1**
MAP L1 ■ 300 Rue Ontario Est

Sip seasonal cocktails – like La Mere Amère, with amaretto, vodka, and grapefruit – from mason jars at this trendy bar. Refuel with fun bar snacks, including jars of gold-fish crackers and buttery popcorn.

**7 Randolph Pub**
MAP L1 ■ 2041 Rue St-Denis

Friendly spot with an expansive collection of ready-to-play board games on the shelves. Good beer and snack menu as well.

**8 Pub Quartier-Latin**
MAP L1 ■ 318 Rue Ontario Est

One of the most comfortable bars in town. There's a lovely terrace, a cozy bar, and a fabulous array of imported and domestic beer.

**9 Pub Le Sainte-Élisabeth**
MAP L2 ■ 1412 Rue Ste-Elisabeth

A renowned pub with a welcoming ambiance, an extensive selection of craft beers on tap, and a secluded garden. It also features one of the finest courtyard terraces in the city, ivy-clad and with a fireplace.

**10 Bar Le Saint-Sulpice**
MAP L1 ■ 1680 Rue St-Denis

A well-known bar especially popular with partying university students. Contemporary music inside and a large garden make for an ideal night out.

*See map on pp68–9*

# Downtown Restaurants

### 1 Otto Yakitori
MAP G1 ▪ 1441 Rue St-Mathieu ▪ (514) 507 8886 ▪ $

Specializing in grilled and skewered meat and vegetables, this quaint and authentic Japanese pub stays open until late in the night.

### 2 Bouillon Bilk
MAP K2 ▪ 1595 Blvd St-Laurent ▪ (514) 845 1595 ▪ www.bouillon bilk.com ▪ $$$

The minimalist setting is a quiet contrast to the French-inspired creativity. Try the braised port with pea ravioli.

### 3 Le Café des Beaux-Arts
MAP C3 ▪ 1384 Rue Sherbrooke Ouest ▪ (514) 843 3233 ▪ www. mbam.qc.ca ▪ $$

French bistro cuisine awaits you inside the luxurious confines of the Musée des Beaux-Arts *(see pp24–5)*. Delicious, creative dishes.

### 4 Les Enfants Terribles
MAP J2 ▪ 44th floor, 1 Place Ville-Marie ▪ www.jesuisunenfant terrible.com ▪ $$

Visit this bustling French brasserie for great food and a stunning view. Try the oysters and the bavette steak.

### 5 Maison Boulud
MAP J1 ▪ 1228 Rue Sherbrooke Ouest ▪ (514) 842 4224 ▪ www.maisonboulud.com ▪ $$$

Helmed by Chef Daniel Boulud, this grand restaurant features French-Québécois cuisine.

**Glitzy dining at Maison Boulud**

### 6 Alpenhaus
MAP B3 ▪ 1279 Rue St-Marc ▪ (514) 935 2285 ▪ www.restaurant alpenhaus.com ▪ $$

The best *wienerschnitzel*, fondue, goulash, and strudel in the city is served here. The Heidi Room can be booked for group celebrations.

### 7 Café Parvis
MAP J1 ▪ 433 Rue Mayor ▪ (514) 764 3589 ▪ www.cafe parvis.com ▪ $$

An oasis in the heart of downtown Montreal. Excellent for brunch, pizzas, and salads to share.

### 8 Taverne F
MAP K2 ▪ 1485 Rue Jeanne-Mance ▪ (514) 289 4558 ▪ www. tavernef.com ▪ $

Dig into dishes like grilled shrimp with garlic and brandy at this bustling restaurant run by the well-known Portuguese chef Carlos Ferreira.

### 9 Fiorellino
MAP J2 ▪ 470 Rue de la Gauchetiére O ▪ (514) 878 3666 ▪ www.fiorellino.ca ▪ $$

Come here for delicious, simple Italian cuisine. The wood-fired pizzas here draw a crowd, but the pasta and desserts are also superb.

### 10 La Habanera
MAP J2 ▪ 1216 Ave Union ▪ (514) 375 5355 ▪ www. lahabanera.ca ▪ $

Colorful Cuban café with small plates to share and excellent cocktails. Try their take on the classic poutine – it's made with yucca.

# Quartier Latin Restaurants

**PRICE CATEGORIES**

For a three-course meal for one with half a bottle of wine (or equivalent meal), taxes and extra charges.

$ under $40 $$ $40–$80 $$$ over $80

###  Le Saloon

MAP M1 ▪ 1333 Rue Ste-Catherine Est ▪ (514) 522 1333 ▪ www.lesaloon.ca ▪ $$

This amiable bistro in the heart of Gay Village serves juicy burgers, hearty sandwiches, fresh salads, and fruity cocktails, along with nachos, poutine, and a lively weekend brunch.

### 2 Restaurant Laloux

MAP D3 ▪ 250 Ave des Pins Est ▪ (514) 287 9127 ▪ www.laloux.com ▪ $$$

Beautifully plated, seasonal French dishes are served at this white-linen bistro. The desserts are superb too.

### 3 Mañana

MAP E3 ▪ 3605 Rue St-Denis ▪ (514) 847 1050 ▪ $$

This Mexican restaurant offers an experience of the country, without falling into the usual clichés. The banana flambé with red wine and tequila is delicious.

### 4 La Relève

MAP E3 ▪ 401 Rue de Rigaud ▪ (514) 282 5161 ▪ www.ithq.qc.ca ▪ $

This is actually a restaurant attached to Canada's leading hotel management school, the ITHQ. The food is varied, of good quality, and the meals are very affordable.

### 5 La Couscoussière d'Ali Baba

MAP M1 ▪ 1460 Rue Amherst ▪ (514) 842 6667 ▪ www.couscoussiere.ca ▪ $$

A Moroccan/Tunisian restaurant serving authentic Middle Eastern fare in an exotic cave-like setting.

### 6 Le Café Cherrier

MAP E3 ▪ 3635 Rue St-Denis ▪ (514) 843 4308 ▪ www.cafe cherrier.ca ▪ $$

This French bistro has one of the best terraces in Montreal, which makes its weekend brunches quite a social event.

Le Café Cherrier

### 7 Uniburger

MAP L1 ▪ 302 Rue Ontario Est ▪ (514) 419 6555 ▪ www.uni burger.com ▪ $

Known for serving the best burgers in Montreal, this legendary, old-fashioned fast food joint is a must-try.

### 8 O'Thym

MAP M1 ▪ 1112 Blvd de Maisonneuve Est (cnr Amherst) ▪ (514) 525 3443 ▪ www.othym.com ▪ $$

This bring-your-own-wine bistro offers dishes based on local ingredients, including venison, salmon, and duck.

### 9 Le Passé Composé

MAP M1 ▪ 1310 Blvd de Maisonneuve Est ▪ (514) 524 6663 ▪ www.bistropassecompose.com ▪ $$

With a reasonably priced *table d'hôte*, this neighborhood French bistro opens for breakfast, lunch, and supper.

### 10 Café Saigon

▪ MAP M1 ▪ 1280 Rue St-André ▪ (514) 849 0429 ▪ $

Popular with the university crowd, this Asian BYO café is famous for its shrimp soup and spring rolls.

*See map on pp68–9*

# TOP 10 Mont-Royal to Hochelaga-Maisonneuve

This generous swath of Montreal includes the most prominent green space and some of the finest attractions of the entire city. The fertile, rolling expanse that makes up Parc du Mont-Royal spreads gracefully into the bustle below – captivating areas such as Little Italy, Rosemont, and Mercier, with a rich ethnic mix flavoring the street life. Here you'll find shops, markets, and restaurants offering every imaginable temptation. For those favoring the outdoor life, the mountain provides an inviting backdrop for a wide range of activities. The Parc Olympique, including the Stade Olympique, Jardin Botanique, and Insectarium, provide visitors, young and old, with an array of entertainment.

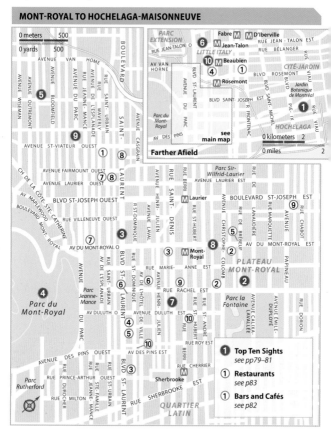

**MONT-ROYAL TO HOCHELAGA-MAISONNEUVE**

| | | | |
|---|---|---|---|
| **1** | **Top Ten Sights** see pp79–81 |
| **1** | **Restaurants** see p83 |
| **1** | **Bars and Cafés** see p82 |

**The Olympic Stadium, the centerpiece of Parc Olympique**

### ① Parc Olympique

This astonishing attraction offers exhilarating activities for all age groups. From the dizzying heights of the world's highest leaning tower, the Tour Montréal atop the Stade Olympique, to the beautiful of the Jardin Botanique, not to mention the awe-inspiring journey through space at the Planétarium Rio Tinto Alcan – you can easily spend a full day or two exploring this area (see pp18–21).

### ② Le Plateau Mont-Royal
MAP E2

Plateau Mont-Royal begins at Rue Sherbrooke and Boulevard Saint-Laurent and spreads northward to Avenue Laurier and east to Parc Lafontaine. This architecturally rich neighborhood was made up of separate villages before being absorbed by the City of Montreal. Ornate duplexes abound on tree-lined streets, where you can see exterior stair-cases, wrought-iron banisters, and fine woodwork. The area is busy day and night with clubs, restaurants, shops, and markets.

### ③ Boulevard Saint-Laurent
MAP D2

East meets west at this long boulevard, referred to as "the Main." Beginning at the waterfront, it designates the symbolic dividing line between the Anglophone west side and the Francophone east side of the city, although in contemporary Montreal this division has all but vanished these days. Here you'll find designer boutiques, chic cafés and sushi bars, gourmet restaurants, and up-to-the-minute nightclubs sometimes stacked two and three floors high, underlining the street's international party reputation. You can buy almost anything you desire here, from cheap clothing to food, antiquarian books, high-tech equipment, diamonds, crafts, kitchenware – even gravestones.

**Parc du Mont-Royal**

### ④ Parc du Mont-Royal

Mont-Royal, after which Montreal is named, defines the city's personality with its year-round outdoor attractions, multi-ethnic cemetery, and lush, rolling breadth above the St Lawrence River. Parc du Mont-Royal has the distinction of being the first place in Quebec to receive historic and natural heritage status, meaning it is protected as a green space (see pp12–13).

**Stalls piled high with fresh produce at the Marché Jean-Talon**

### 5 Outremont
MAP C1

Founded in 1695, this area, meaning "beyond the mountain," is the predominantly French-speaking wealthy residential quarter. It features some of the most luxurious mansions in the city, and the main thoroughfares of Avenue Laurier and Rue Bernard west of Avenue du Parc are peppered with expensive fashion boutiques, exclusive hair salons, and hip eateries serving a clientele more akin to Paris than North America. Don't miss one of the country's finest *fromageries* (cheese-makers), Fromagerie Yannick (1218 Rue Bernard), or the rich pastries at Hof Kelsten (4524 Blvd St-Laurent). You can get lost in this area due to the meandering streets, so keep a mental note of your route.

### 6 Marché Jean-Talon
Métro Jean-Talon

A walk through the alluring Marché Jean-Talon tempts the senses with a profusion of fresh market fare, imported Italian gourmet luxuries, and homemade marvels from traditional local kitchens. Fresh produce is brought to market daily by dozens of farmers from outlying regions, together with discerning local importers. Also inside the market area is the Marché des Saveurs du Québec, a market within a market, which departs from the Italian theme and presents a line-up of specialties from Quebec Province.

---

**MAISON DE LA CULTURE**

Montreal has one of the most prized cultural networks in the world, evident in a system of venues called Maison de la Culture (house of culture) where music, art, and symposia are offered to the public for free or at minimal cost. The best example is the Chapelle Historique du Bon-Pasteur at 100 Rue Sherbrooke Est, which has now become a concert hall.

---

### 7 Rue Saint-Denis
MAP E2

Architectural treasures, street poets, clothing stores, and a plethora of restaurants and cafés are the main attractions on this street. From Old Montreal's Carré Viger north to Carré Saint-Louis, the Victorian architecture seems to blend effortlessly with the designer

**Vibrant Rue Saint-Denis**

stores, hip-hop music culture, and the buzzing youthful vitality that is the essence of this area.

## Avenue du Mont-Royal
MAP D2

This street has vitality and panache, reflected in its bevy of eclectic eateries, curiosity shops, and cafés, but mostly in the laid-back attitude of its residents. Bargain shops nestle beside boutiques, while markets sell everything from fashion to ethnic food.

## Avenue du Parc
MAP D2

Starting at Rue Sherbrooke heading north, this riotous thoroughfare slices through the principal neighborhoods of the city. You can spend a whole day on this one street alone: enjoying the Tam-Tam drum festival (Sundays only), sampling an authentic Greek, Lebanese or Italian lunch, shopping for bargains or custom-made leather coats in the afternoon, then stopping for a swim at the YMCA, and finally enjoying a drink while listening to live African music.

**Tam-Tam festival, Avenue du Parc**

## Little Italy
Métro Jean-Talon

Italian Canadians offer another side to Montreal's ethnic blend and make up the largest immigrant community, tracing their presence in the city back to the early 19th century. Boulevard Saint-Laurent provides the Italian version of café society in a stream of cafés and restaurants, but Little Italy proper is defined by the borders of Rue Jean-Talon, Rue Saint-Zotique, Rue Marconi, and Avenue Drolet. Nudging up against Little Italy is the arty neighborhood of Mile-Ex.

### A DAY'S WALK AROUND MONT-ROYAL

### MORNING

Take the No. 11 bus from Mont-Royal Métro station up Avenue du Mont-Royal and you will be able to see the **Parc Olympique** (see pp18–21) to the east. Disembark at **Lac aux Castors** (see p13) and walk around the lakeside trail to see resident ducks and geese. Follow the trail, veering to your left, to Chemin Olmsted, which leads you past sculptures of the International Sculpture Symposium. Continue to **Maison Smith** (see p13), and take in the wonderful exhibit presented by Les Amis de la Montagne (Friends of the Mountain).

Return to Chemin Olmsted and follow the trail left to the commemorative Olmsted plaque embedded in rock, and then on to the main chalet and **Kondiaronk Lookout** (see p12), the best viewpoint of the city. Return to the path behind the chalet, turn right and a little farther on, climb the path on your left to the foot of **La Croix** (see p12), the most recognized symbol of Montreal.

Return to Maison Smith to take the bus back to Mont-Royal station, and then head to nearby Beautys (93 av du Mont-Royal Ouest), a beloved 1950s diner – try the bagel with eggs, bacon, and cheese. Then stroll east on buzzing Avenue du Mont-Royal.

### AFTERNOON

You can either spend the afternoon enjoying some of the best shopping in the area on Avenue Duluth, or relax in the lovely Parc Lafontaine (see p46).

*See map on p78* ←

# Bars and Cafés

### **1** Café Olimpico
MAP D1

■ 124 Rue St-Viateur Ouest

Founded in 1970, this phenomenally popular Italian café in the uber-hip Mile End district is packed with regulars who swear that its lattes are the city's best.

**Café Olimpico**

### **2** Barraca Rhumerie et Tapas
MAP E2 ■ 1134 Ave du Mont-Royal Est

This tightly packed spot is popular with young people who have a penchant for rum. Dozens of brands from 11 countries are served alongside delicious tapas.

### **3** Bílý Kůň
MAP E2

■ 354 Ave du Mont-Royal Est

Busy Czech microbrewery with live jazz, classical performances, and DJs. Good bar snacks too.

### **4** Isle De Garde
MAP E1

■ 1039 Rue Beaubien Est

This cozy bar pours an innovative array of beer, from Berliner Melon Weisse (from Dunham, Quebec) to dry, tart ciders, and the house-made Isle de Garde Brown Porter ale.

### **5** Café Rico
MAP E2 ■ 1215 Ave du Mont-Royal Est

Established over a decade ago, this friendly café and bean roaster serves organic and certified fair-trade coffee, along with fresh pastries and sandwiches.

### **6** Café Néve
MAP D2 ■ 151 Rue Rachel Est

This is the flagship location of the artisanal coffee chain founded in Montreal. It offers coffee lovers a wonderful ambiance to go with its famous cookies. Brunch is served until 2pm every day, and includes eggs benedict, *croque monsieur*, and various tartines.

### **7** Bar Henrietta
MAP D1 ■ 115 Ave Laurier Ouest

Enjoy Portuguese-tavern-inspired food at this bustling restaurant. There is also an extensive cocktail and wine list.

### **8** Sparrow
MAP D1 ■ 5322 Blvd St-Laurent

With an eclectic background music selection, this casual cocktail bar has a warm and vintage feel to it. Try their weekend brunch, which pairs well with the excellent beers on tap.

### **9** El Zaz Bar
MAP E2 ■ 4297 Rue St-Denis

A psychedelic landmark in Montreal's Plateau district, the El Zaz Bar hosts musical acts of all types. They also have DJs who are up spinning tunes seven nights a week.

### **10** Else's
MAP E2 ■ 156 Rue Roy Est

This favored neighborhood bar for musicians, artists, and bohemians serves a homey menu of juicy burgers, sausages, and shrimp tacos, and signature breads.

# Restaurants

**PRICE CATEGORIES**

For a three-course meal for one with half a bottle of wine (or equivalent meal), taxes and extra charges.

......................................................

**$** under $40   **$$** $40–$80   **$$$** over $80

### 1 Larry's
MAP D1 ■ 9 Ave Fairmount Est ■ $$

This charming neighborhood eatery has an eclectic menu, an extensive wine list, and great cocktails. Don't miss the delicious homemade bread.

### 2 Ty-Breiz Crêperie Bretonne
MAP E2 ■ 933 Rue Rachel Est ■ (514) 521 1444 ■ $

Step into this perennial favorite and taste Bretonne food in its traditional forms, from onion soup and frog's legs to the assortment of crêpes.

### 3 Maestro SVP
MAP D2 ■ 3615 Blvd St-Laurent ■ (514) 842 6447 ■ $$

This is the place for oysters. Try them fresh, baked, or in a shooter with vodka and horseradish sauce.

### 4 Moishe's
MAP D2 ■ 3961 Blvd St-Laurent ■ (514) 845 3509 ■ $$$

This steakhouse has been attracting businesspeople for years with their steaks topped with dill pickles.

**Dining room at Moishe's**

### 5 Schwartz's
MAP D2 ■ 3895 Blvd St-Laurent ■ (514) 842 4813 ■ $

Few things are as distinctly Montreal as this landmark Hebrew delicatessen. Its smoked meat sandwiches are world-famous.

**Smoked meat sandwich, Schwartz's**

### 6 Patati Patata Friterie Deluxe
MAP D2 ■ 4177 Blvd St-Laurent ■ (514) 844 0216 ■ $

A little, budget-friendly burger joint that also serves a classic poutine, crêpes, and fresh juices.

### 7 Le Filet
MAP D2 ■ 219 Ave du Mont-Royal Ouest ■ (514) 360 6060 ■ $$

At this sleek seafood restaurant the fresh fish and shellfish shine, with minimal but well-selected garnishes.

### 8 Wilensky's Light Lunch
MAP D1 ■ 34 Ave Fairmont Ouest ■ (514) 271 0247 ■ Closed Sun ■ $

Deli serving cream sodas and grilled salami, bologna, and Swiss-cheese sandwiches since 1932.

### 9 Le Pégase
1831 Rue Gilford ■ (514) 522 0487 ■ $$

Bring your own wine to complement the French food at this small bistro.

### 10 Au Pied De Cochon
MAP E2 ■ 536 Ave Duluth Est ■ (514) 281 1114 ■ $$

A meat-centric restaurant where the chef, Martin Picard, has a playful approach to Québécois cuisine.

*See map on p78*

# TOP 10 Excursions from Montreal

On Friday nights and Saturday mornings Montreal's bridges are crowded with residents traveling out of town to enjoy the activities possible in the surrounding countryside. Les Laurentides (the Laurentian mountains) and the Cantons-de-l'Est (the Eastern Townships) are where Montrealers venture to hike in summer or ski in winter. Traffic through the locks at Sainte-Anne-de-Bellevue also buzzes with boaters heading west on the Ottawa River or east to Trois-Rivières, Quebec City, and on to the Atlantic Ocean. Beaches at Parc National d'Oka, Lac Memphrémagog, or Lac des Sables draw sun-lovers in summer.

**Caribou, Parc Oméga, Outaouais**

## EXCURSIONS FROM MONTREAL

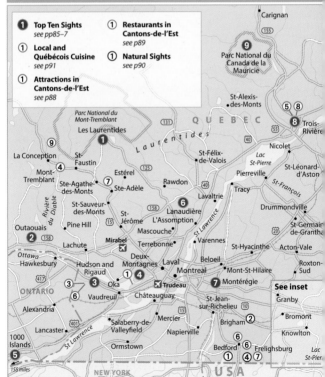

1 Top Ten Sights *see pp85–7*

1 Local and Québécois Cuisine *see p91*

1 Attractions in Cantons-de-l'Est *see p88*

1 Restaurants in Cantons-de-l'Est *see p89*

1 Natural Sights *see p90*

**Mont Tremblant village buried in the Laurentian mountains**

### 1 Les Laurentides

Only an hour from the congestion of Montreal, the stunning Laurentian mountains north of the city provide an astounding list of activities. In summer there are endless opportunities to swim, fish, raft, horse-ride, play golf, mountain climb, or just relax in the sunny rural setting. Winter brings the chance to ski (downhill or cross-country), go tobogganing or snowboarding (see pp36–7).

### 2 Outaouais

MAP N5 ▪ Oméga Park: 399 Rte 323 N ▪ Manoir Louis-Joseph-Papineau: 500 Rue Notre-Dame, Montebello; Open May & Jun: 10am–5pm Fri & Sat, Jul & Aug: 10am–5pm daily, Sep & Oct: 10am–5pm Fri–Sun; Adm

This historic area west of Montreal was not settled by white people until the early 19th century, and it remains largely undeveloped. Don't miss Oméga Safari Park, just outside Montebello, with its 1,500 acres (607 ha) inhabited by roaming bison, wapitis, black bear, and wolves, then continue on to the Parc National de Plaisance along the Ottawa River, to see flocks of Canada geese. In Montebello itself visit Manoir Louis-Joseph-Papineau, a 19th-century home filled with antiques and local artifacts.

### 3 Hudson and Rigaud

MAP N6

A favorite jaunt west from Montreal, the communities of Hudson and Rigaud hug the mountains along the pastoral Ottawa River. Hudson, with its history of British settlement and fur trading, has historic mansions set on magnificent estates and an abundance of antiques shops, art galleries, and cafés. Its landscape is popular for equestrians, while its riverside setting draws a sailing crowd. The village of Rigaud is more French, maintaining its Gallic legacy in churches and family-run farms.

**10 Cantons-de-l'Est**

Granby
Sherbrooke
Waterloo
North Hatley
Bromont
Magog
Knowlton
W Brome
Coaticook

0 km   10
0 miles   10

Princeville
Plessisville
Thetford Mines
Victoriaville
La Guadeloupe
Chesterville
Saint-Joseph-de-Coleraine
Warwick
Beaulac
Stornoway
Richmond
Dudswell
Gould
Laval-Nord
Scotstown
La Patrie
Sherbrooke
Saint-Isidore-de-Clifton
Magog
Compton
MAINE
Coaticook
NEW HAMPSHIRE
VERMONT

0 km   25
0 miles   25

**BRIDGES OF MONTREAL**

Getting on and off the island city of Montreal can be daunting. Pay due respect to the French *"pont"* (bridge) signage, because once you are on a bridge, you must continue across it before you can turn around. There are a total of 18 bridges and one tunnel providing access to the city.

### 4 Deux-Montagnes
MAP N6 ■ www.ville.deux-montagnes.qc.ca

This community, 30 minutes' drive from Montreal, was first settled by the Sulpician Order during the French Regime, and the fresh produce of this region, including the famous Oka cheese, is a carry-over from the agricultural traditions begun by the priests. Parc National d'Oka offers camping, kayaking, hiking, and a sandy beach.

### 5 1000 Islands
Rte No. 401 ■ Boat trips: St Lawrence Cruise Lines: 1-800 267 7868 ■ www.stlawrencerivercruise.com

These islands are a great escape, accessible either by car or train to Brockville. About 2 hours west of the border of Ontario and Quebec, 1000 Islands actually covers 1,865 islands running the 50-mile (80-km) span from Brockville to Kingston, and were formed by metamorphic rock at the end of the last Ice Age. Thousand Islands National Park is the *pièce de résistance* with 21 main islands, most of which have camping facilities.

**Bonaventure Island, 1000 Islands**

### 6 Lanaudière
MAP P5 ■ www.lanaudiere.ca

From the St Lawrence River Valley rising to the Laurentian lowland plateau, there's a multitude of forests, lakes, rivers, and farmland to explore in this region, all within a few hours of Montreal. You can enjoy numerous activities here, indoors and out. The Festival de Lanaudière, Canada's most renowned classical music festival, takes place from early June to early August, with concerts staged at outdoor venues and heritage churches in Joliette.

**Waterfall, Lanaudière**

### 7 Montérégie
MAP P5 ■ www.tourisme-monteregie.qc.ca ■ Fort Chambly: 2 Rue Richelieu, Chambly ■ Open May–Oct: 10am–5pm Wed–Sun (Jun–Sep: daily; Jul–Aug: to 6pm) ■ Adm

To reach this huge region of plains, forests, and history, drive across the Pont Champlain, following signs for highway 10 eastward. Then take highway 133 (also called Chemin des Patriotes after the soldiers who fought the British here in 1837) toward Sorel, one of the oldest cities in Canada. Boat trips are possible around the town's many islands. Of major note in the region, which is known for its apple orchards and cider-making, is Fort Chambly. This well-preserved 18th-century fortress was built to defend the French from both Dutch and British attack.

### 8 Trois-Rivières
MAP Q5

Sieur de Laviolette founded this community in 1634, but the beautiful French Regime architecture that once graced the streets was ravaged by a monstrous fire that swept through the entire town in 1908. Only remnants of the original wall survive. Today the town is known as one of the main providers of pulp and paper in the world. Dominating the landscape is the Monastère des Ursulines, a lovely church built by Ursuline nuns, surrounded by a public park. There are a plethora of cafés, bistros, and restaurants on Rue des Forges.

### 9 Parc National du Canada de la Mauricie

MAP P4 ■ Adm ■ www.pc.gc.ca

One of Canada's most spectacular areas of rivers, lakes, mountains, and wildlife, La Mauricie National Park is only a two-hour drive from downtown Montreal or Quebec City. It is accessible all year round, and is a perennial favorite with campers and outdoor enthusiasts. It is particularly popular with anglers, with trout and pike found in abundance in Lac Wapizagonke.

Canoeing, La Mauricie National Park

### 10 Cantons-de-l'Est

MAP Q6

■ www.cantonsdelest.com

This natural wonderland is bounded by the Richelieu and St Lawrence rivers and the US states of Vermont, New Hampshire, and Maine. The biggest feature is the Appalachian Mountains, with top-notch hiking trails at Owl's Head, Mont Sutton, Mont Bromont, and Mont Orford. The villages of this vast district, such as Knowlton, are a remnant of 19th-century British settlement, their Victorian buildings now home to antiques shops and cafés (see pp88–9).

---

## A DAY IN VAL-DAVID AND THE P'TIT TRAIN DU NORD TRAIL

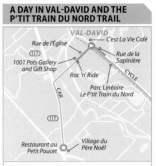

### ▶ MORNING

Take Route 15, the Laurentian Autoroute, north to Exit 76, then join Route 117 north to the village of **Val-David** (see p37). At the Municipalité de Val-David (2501 Rue de l'Église) you can obtain a map and detailed information about the region.

Walk down **Rue de l'Église** to visit the **1001 Pots Gallery and Gift Shop** (2435 Rue de l'Église). This exhibition of handmade pottery and works of art is one of the largest ceramic shows in North America, produced by an esteemed collective of over 50 Québécois artists. For a great lunch, backtrack to Rue de la Sapinière and turn left to C'est La Vie Café (1347 Rue de la Sapinière; (819) 320 0273).

### AFTERNOON

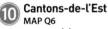

After lunch, explore the **Parc Linéaire Le P'tit Train du Nord** (see p48), a green swath of protected trails snaking 144 miles (232 km) through the Laurentides on the old mountain train path. The defunct railroad line is perfect for hiking, cycling, and walking in summer and cross-country skiing in winter. If cycling is your preference, Roc 'n' Ride (2444 Rue de l'Église) rents bikes.

Return to Val-David and, if you have the energy, shop for unusual Christmas decorations at **Village du Père Noël** (987 Rue Morin), open all year. Then enjoy a Québécois dinner at **Restaurant au Petit Poucet** (see p91).

See map on pp84–5

# Attractions in Cantons-de-l'Est

 **Zoo de Granby**
MAP Q6 ▪ 1050 Blvd David-Bouchard, Granby ▪ Opening times vary (check www.zoodegranby.com for details) ▪ Adm

This zoo is home to over 225 species of animals from around the globe.

 **Parc National du Mont-Orford**

MAP Q6 ▪ 3321 Chemin du Parc, Canton d'Orford

Rising majestically beside the Eastern Townships Autoroute, Mont Orford is the central area for outdoor activities in this sprawling preserve, covering over 22 sq miles (57 sq km) around the mountain.

 **Knowlton**
MAP Q6

Set on the inviting shores of Lac Brome, this 19th-century Anglophone village has an idyllic locale, attracting vacationers.

 **Lac Memphrémagog**
MAP Q6

This huge lake is a draw for boat-lovers. Legend has it that the lake is home to a "memphre" – a long-necked, dark green reptilian monster that has apparently been sighted over 200 times since 1847.

 **L'Abbaye de Saint-Benoît-du-Lac**

MAP Q6 ▪ Saint-Benoît-du-Lac ▪ Open 5am–9pm daily

Benedictine monks founded this monastery overlooking Lac Memphrémagog in 1912. Gregorian chants take place daily at 7:30am, 11am, and 5pm.

 **Le Chemin des Vignobles de l'Estrie**
MAP P6

Due to its slate soil and climate this area has a highly respected wine-growing tradition visible along the Wine Route (Hwy 202) between Dunham and Stanbridge East.

 **Frelighsburg**
MAP P6

A peaceful town at the foot of Mount Pinnacle and near the US border, Frelighsburg's landscape attracts artists and photographers.

**Fall landscape around Frelighsburg**

 **Bromont**
MAP Q6 ▪ Le Musée de Chocolat: 679 Rue Shefford; 8:30am–6pm Mon–Fri, 8am–5:30pm Sat & Sun

Bromont embodies all the best of Cantons-de-l'Est: A quaint main street is lined with antique shops and galleries; cozy restaurants serve farm-fresh cuisine; and the town is surrounded by the great outdoors. For a sweet visit stop into the Musée du Chocolat, where you can learn about chocolate-making while nibbling on fine specimens.

 **Sherbrooke**
MAP Q6

The Rivière Saint-François bisects this commercial center of Cantons-de-l'Est. Despite its history of British settlement, today it is predominantly a French-speaking town.

 **Parc de la Gorge de Coaticook**
MAP Q6

This park is set around a 165-ft (50-m) gorge, and offers hiking trails and horse riding, as well snow and ice activities in winter (see p90).

# Restaurants in Cantons-de-l'Est

**PRICE CATEGORIES**

For a three-course meal for one with half a bottle of wine (or equivalent meal), taxes and extra charges

**$** under $40 **$$** $40–$80 **$$$** over $80

### ① Café Massawippi
MAP Q6 ▪ 3050 Chemin Capelton, North Hatley ▪ (819) 842 4528 ▪ Closed Sun & Mon (Nov–May) ▪ $$$

The food and service are the stuff of dreams in this welcoming house. The locally-inspired menu includes foie gras, duck poutine, and venison.

### ② Haut Bois Normand
MAP Q6 ▪ 426 Chemin George-Bonnallie, Eastman ▪ (450) 297 2659 ▪ Open weekends only ▪ $

Experience adventure trails in summer and tubing in winter before sampling traditional Québécois fare. In March, try the *tire sur neige* (maple-syrup taffy on snow).

### ③ Auberge aux Toits Rouges
MAP off Q6 ▪ 72 Rue Chesham, Notre-Dame-des-Bois ▪ (819) 888 2999 ▪ $$

Local produce features highly at this country inn. One of the highlights is the *filet mignon*.

### ④ Siboire
MAP Q6 ▪ 80 Rue du Dépôt, Sherbrooke ▪ (819) 565 3636 ▪ $

Set in a former train station, this spacious microbrewery is known for its excellent fish and chips. The adjoining terrace is lovely on warmer days.

### ⑤ Auberge West Brome
MAP Q6 ▪ 128 Rte 139, West Brome ▪ (450) 266 7552 ▪ $$$

Luxurious Auberge West Brome offers Lac Brome duck and other regional specialties, grown in the on-site organic vegetable garden, as well as first-class accommodations.

### ⑥ L'Oeuf
MAP P6 ▪ 229 Chemin Mystic, Mystic ▪ (450) 248 7529 ▪ Closed Mon & Tue ▪ $$

A gourmet restaurant, *chocolaterie*, and auberge specializing in creative dishes, ending with chocolate.

### ⑦ Le Cellier Du Roi Par Jérôme Ferrer
MAP Q6 ▪ Le Royal Bromont, 400 Chemin Compton ▪ (450) 534 4653 ▪ $$$

Amid the grounds of Le Royal Bromont golf course, Chef Jérôme Ferrer showcases his Quebec-inspired cuisine with a menu deeply rooted in the region.

**Le Cellier Du Roi Par Jérôme Ferrer**

### ⑧ Pinocchio
MAP Q6 ▪ 469 Rue Principale Ouest, Magog ▪ (819) 868 8808 ▪ $$

This chic, white-linen restaurant offers fresh meat and seafood dishes. The wine list is excellent.

### ⑨ La Table du Chef
MAP Q6 ▪ 11 Rue Victoria, Sherbrooke ▪ (819) 562 2258 ▪ $$

Run by renowned chef Alain Labrie, this stylish restaurant excels at French-accented regional cuisine, including grilled bison and wild boar.

### ⑩ Auberge du Joli Vent
MAP Q6 ▪ 667 Chemin Bondville, Lac-Brome ▪ (450) 243 4272 ▪ Open Fri & Sat dinner only (Jul–Aug Thu also) ▪ $$

A weekly changing menu features innovative dishes using locally sourced seasonal ingredients.

*See map on pp84–5*→

# Natural Sights

 **Missisquoi Bay**
MAP P6

The traditional home of the Abenaki native people, this lush area in the western corner of Cantons-de-l'Est was the first refuge for Loyalist settlers crossing into Canada after the American Revolution.

 **The Orchards**
MAP Q6

The best territory for apples in the province is the Montérégie Region, but Cantons-de-l'Est also has plenty of orchards around Dunham, Brigham, Compton, and Stanbridge.

 **Lac Brome**
MAP Q6

Lac Brome has several delightful lakeside communities: Knowlton, Foster, Bondville, Fulford, Iron Hill, East Hill, and West Brome – all retain in part a bygone way of life.

 **Route Saint-Armand**
MAP Q6

In 1748 the Seigneurie Saint-Armand was given to René-Nicholas Levasseur by the King of France. Much of this grand property can be seen today on the roads from Vale Perkins on Lac Memphrémagog to Saint-Armand.

**5** **Mont Sutton**
MAP Q6

Since it opened in 1960, Mont Sutton has been a favorite with downhill skiers due to its superior slopes.

 **Mont Owl's Head**
MAP Q6

Set above Lac Memphrémagog, this ski resort has a vertical drop of 1,770 ft (540 m). An annual autumn music festival is held at the end of September.

 **Lac Massawippi**
MAP Q6

Celebrities on the list of regulars at the Manoir Hovey resort here (see p113). Le Festival du Lac Massawippi runs popular music concerts from June until the end of August.

**8** **Parc de la Gorge de Coaticook**
MAP Q6

Over 50,000 years ago the Wisconsin Glacier started to melt, giving birth to the Coaticook Lake and then this river, which dug a cavernous gorge. It now attracts visitors to the longest pedestrian suspension bridge in North America (see p88).

**9** **Parc National du Mont-Mégantic**
Rte No. 257

Stargazing is the rule in this huge natural wonderland as the Astrolab beckons astronomers of every level.

**10** **Lac Mégantic**
Rte No. 161

Located at the eastern edge of the townships in the Appalachian foothills, this peaceful lake provides outdoor activities and has a beach.

**Riding the chairlift to the top of Mont Sutton**

# Local and Québécois Cuisine

**PRICE CATEGORIES**

For a three-course meal for one with half a bottle of wine (or equivalent meal), taxes and extra charges.

$ under $40   $$ $40–$80   $$$ over $80

### 1 Cap Saint-Jacques Maison de la Ferme Ecologique

MAP N6 ▪ 183 Chemin du Cap-Saint-Jacques, Pierrefonds ▪ (514) 280 6743 ▪ Closed D ▪ $

Visit this large organic farm and meet the chickens, taste the local maple syrup and honey, and pick up fresh vegetables and preserves from the on-site store.

### 2 Owl's Bread Bakery

MAP Q6 ▪ 299A Rue Principale, Mansonville ▪ (450) 292 3088 ▪ $

This artisanal French bakery is also a high-end grocery and bistro. Almost all ingredients are organic and local.

### 3 Sucrerie de la Montagne

MAP N6 ▪ 300 St Georges Rd, Rigaud ▪ (450) 451 0831 ▪ $$

Pierre Faucher's maple sugar house serves Québécois cuisine such as pea soup, *tourtière* (meat pie), wood-fired baked beans, maple-glazed smoked ham, and maple sugar pie.

### 4 Le Cheval de Jade

MAP N5 ▪ 688 Rue de Saint-Jovite, Mont Tremblant ▪ (819) 425 5233 ▪ $$$

This is a place of refined pleasures. Chef Olivier Tali crafts delectable French-influenced Québécois fare. Try the table-side flambéed Duck à la Rouennaise for two.

### 5 Le Lupin

MAP Q5 ▪ 376 Rue St-Georges, Trois-Rivières ▪ (819) 370 4740 ▪ $$

An inviting "bring your own bottle" restaurant serving home-style local dishes, from sweet and savoury crepes to mussels and steaks.

### 6 Ferme Apicole Intermiel

MAP N5 ▪ 10291 rang de la Fresnière, Mirabel ▪ (450) 258 2713 ▪ Closed D ▪ $

This farm offers wonderful picnic sites with an abundance of apiary products to taste afterwards, such as honey mead and honey cookies.

**Honey bees, Ferme Apicole Intermiel**

### 7 Restaurant au Petit Poucet

MAP N5 ▪ 1030 Rte 117, Val David ▪ (819) 322 2246 ▪ $$

Find mouth-watering, maple-smoked ham, meat pies, and sugar pies at this rustic cottage established in 1945.

### 8 Poivre Noir

MAP Q5 ▪ 1300 Rue du Fleuve, Trois-Rivières ▪ (819) 378 5772 ▪ $$$

Dig into dishes crafted in Québécois style, from bison tartare to rich foie gras with smoked apple.

### 9 Le Petite Cachée

MAP N5 ▪ 2681 Chemin du Village, Mont Tremblant ▪ (819) 425 2654 ▪ $$$

Known for its traditional French and Québécois cuisine, Le Petite Cachée is a charming bistro. Try the braised beef ribs or the pan-seared Arctic char.

### 10 Restaurant L'Imperial

MAP Q6 ▪ 320 Blvd Leclerc, Local 28, Granby ▪ (450) 994 1922 ▪ Closed Mon ▪ $$$

Run by renowned chef Jean-Philippe Tastet, this destination eatery serves delicious duck bolognese ravioli, pistachio-stuffed rabbit, and indulgent desserts. Extensive wine list.

*See map on pp84–5*

# 🔟 Quebec City

**Shop at Petit-Champlain**

Europeans first settled here in 1608, and throughout its history Quebec City has been the focus of political struggle between the British and the French – a battle that still rages today in this home of French separatism. Yet despite this turmoil, with its beautiful riverside setting, heritage sites, and cobblestone streets – all of which earned it World Heritage status in 1985 – the city is a traveler's dream. Poised upon the Cap Diamant escarpment overlooking the St Lawrence River and Les Laurentides, the city is home to a Francophone population rich in cultural pride and exuberance, magnificent architecture, preserved churches and monuments, fine cuisine, and numerous opportunities for outdoor adventure.

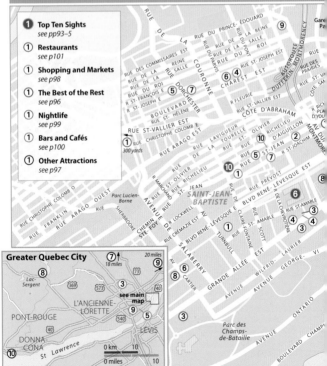

**QUEBEC CITY**

1 **Top Ten Sights**
see pp93–5

① **Restaurants**
see p101

① **Shopping and Markets**
see p98

① **The Best of the Rest**
see p96

① **Nightlife**
see p99

① **Bars and Cafés**
see p100

① **Other Attractions**
see p97

**Greater Quebec City**

**Aerial view, La Citadelle**

### 1 La Citadelle

Strategically perched on the precipice of Cap Diamant with a full 360-degree view, this powerful bastion would daunt the bravest of enemies approaching the riverside city. All you need to do is attend one of its summertime cannon-firing demonstrations to appreciate the persuasive power of this mighty fortress (see pp28–9).

### 2 Musée de la Civilisation de Québec

Architect Moishe Safdie mirrored the surrounding neighborhood by incorporating the French Regime style in his design for this interesting building. Inside, however, it is another story – a futuristic world complete with a range of interactive exhibitions, as well as displays of folk art, religious icons, antique furniture in period settings, and everyday items that illustrate life in the city during its 400-year history. There are also collaborative exhibitions at the Musée de l'Amérique Francophone, the extra space allowing for a comprehensive program covering multiple themes and generations (see pp30–31).

### 3 Château Frontenac

The most photographed landmark in the city, this hotel with its green copper roof is an architectural jewel designed by architect Bruce Price as a French-style château. Since it opened in 1893, the hotel has welcomed the rich, the famous, and the noble through its doors and into its plush salons. Guided tours are available (see p112).

**The imposing Château Frontenac**

**TROMPE-L'OEIL**

*Trompe-l'oeil* means "to deceive the eye" and if you are in the Quartier Saint-Roch district of Quebec City (near the train station) you can see a marvelous example of this art tradition on the columns on Rue Charest Est. Combining the energetic talents of street graffiti artists under the guidance of a trained painter, a project evolved creating *trompe l'oeil* paintings to decorate cement highway pillars. The results are astounding and have led to the graffiti artists forming their own legitimate company.

### 4 Quartier Petit-Champlain

**MAP M5**

Home to 17th-century artisans and dockworkers, the houses in this area have now been renovated and adapted into an attractive range of eclectic gift shops, transforming what is the oldest part of the city into today's liveliest quarter. Maple butter, French macramé, and sculpted cherrywood cribs are just a few of the many unusual treats you can purchase here. Along the way you can eat and drink in the bars and cafés lining the pedestrianized streets.

### 5 Parc des Champs-de-Bataille

**MAP K6 ■ Open 9am–5:30pm daily ■ Adm**

Designed to commemorate both French and British soldiers, the Plains of Abraham Museum is located within one of the park's many historic buildings and offers an inventive agenda to illustrate one of North America's most historic sites. The highlight is a multimedia show recounting the battles of 1759 and 1760 that took place here, and which led to a French defeat by the British *(see p40)*. An imposing mural by Quebec artist Aline Martineau depicts the establishment of the park in the 1930s and how it has changed over the years *(see p47)*.

### 6 Observatoire de la capitale

**MAP J6 ■ 1037 Rue de la Chevrotière ■ Open 10am–5pm daily (closed Mon mid-Oct–Jan) ■ Adm**

From the 31st floor of the Capital Observatory you can enjoy spectacular views of the entire area. Adding to the experience are the taped interpretation guides offering interesting information about the city in French, English, and Spanish. You can also learn about many aspects of the city's history at the interactive Horizons exhibit. Many city tours begin or end here too.

### 7 Place Royale

**MAP M5**

The site of Nouvelle-France's first settlement, built by Samuel de Champlain in 1608, has been the hub of the city's cultural activities throughout its history. Shipbuilders, merchants, clergy, and everyday citizens once gathered here to conduct commerce, celebrate harvests, marry, drink, and bury their dead. Today, festivals such as Les Fêtes de la Nouvelle-France *(see p57)* rekindle the days of the early settlers with theatrical performances and traditional music. Don't miss Église Notre-Dame-des-Victoires, which has a collection of paintings by Van Dyck depicting the French victory over the British in 1690 *(see p31)*.

**Notre-Dame-des-Victoires, Place Royale**

### 8  Place de l'Hôtel de Ville
MAP L5

In the 18th century this square was the site of the Notre-Dame market and is still a popular gathering place for locals. During the summer it is often jammed with visitors who come to enjoy free music concerts and performances by local actors. The Romanesque architecture, as seen in the Hôtel de Ville (town hall) immediately beside the square, lends the area an imposing air.

Place de l'Hôtel de Ville

### 9  Marché du Vieux-Port
MAP L4 ■ 160 quai St-André

The Bassin Louise is the home of the Old Town's fresh produce market, where farmers from Île d'Orléans (see pp34–5) and other outlying areas bring their harvest to tempt appetites and inspire local chefs. Don't be afraid to ask for a sample before you buy, especially at La Fromagère cheese stall. Inside the green-roofed building is a café, where you can savor more of the local delights.

### 10  Faubourg Saint-Jean-Baptiste
MAP H5

Built as a military defence against the British in the 18th century, the striking stone gate (Porte Saint-Jean) is a tourist draw from which visitors can walk for 3 miles (4 km) along the city's ramparts. The area around the gate, also known as Quartier Montcalm, has a concentration of Québécois specialty merchants, as well as designer boutiques, cultural outlets, and nightclubs. This zone is famous for its bistros and restaurants serving fine French cuisine.

---

**A DAY EXPLORING THE OLD TOWN**

#### ▶ MORNING

Start your day at **Château Frontenac** (see p93) for a breathtaking view of the St Lawrence River, Basse-Ville, Vieux-Port, and Île d'Orléans (see pp34–5) in the distance. Immediately beside the hotel runs **Terrasse-Dufferin** (see p97), a boardwalk clinging to the rock escarpment complete with ornate Parisian-style street lamps. After taking in the exhilarating surroundings, stroll through the **Jardins des Gouverneurs** and look for monuments to Wolfe and Montcalm, the French and English generals in the Battle of the Plains of Abraham (see p40).

Go back along Terrasse-Dufferin to **Quartier Petit-Champlain**, the oldest merchant district in North America, with its dazzling variety of boutiques and souvenir shops.

Enjoy hearty local fare, like rabbit lasagne and cheese fondue, at the inviting **Lapin Sauté** (52 Rue du Petit-Champlain).

#### AFTERNOON

If you want to stretch your legs after lunch, follow the natural flow of the land to the waterfront, head left along **Rue Dalhousie** and the Vieux-Port and turn left at **Rue St-André**. Here you'll find the delights of **Marché du Vieux-Port**, where you could easily spend the rest of the afternoon, sampling the local treats.

For an early evening cocktail and, perhaps, a bite of something fresh and local, head over to **Chez Rioux & Pettigrew** (160 Rue St-Paul).

See map on pp92–3 ←

# The Best of the Rest

**(1) Place D'Youville**
MAP K5

This popular square, located in front of the 18th-century stone gate Porte Saint-Jean, bustles with activity. Outdoor music concerts are held here in summer and there is an ice-skating rink from October to March.

**(2) Sanctuaire Notre-Dame du Sacré-Coeur**
MAP L5 ■ 71 Rue Ste-Ursule ■ Open 7am–8pm daily

Stained-glass windows and marble plaques are highlights of this Neo-Gothic jewel, built in 1910.

**(3) Musée National des Beaux-Arts du Québec**
MAP K6 ■ 179 Grande Allée Ouest ■ Open 10am–6pm Tue–Sun (to 9pm Wed; to 5pm Labor Day–May) ■ Adm

These four distinct pavilions (including a former jailhouse) exhibit works by Québécois and international artists.

**(4) Morrin Centre**
MAP L5 ■ 44 Chaussée des Écossais ■ Open noon–4pm Wed–Sun & noon–8pm Tue ■ Adm

Historic site with guided tours taking you through 18th-century prisons.

Quebec City to Lévis Ferry

**(5) Quebec City to Lévis Ferry**
MAP M5 ■ 10 Rue des Traversiers

This 10-minute crossing offers a stunning view of the city.

Porte Saint-Louis

**(6) Porte Saint-Louis**
MAP K5

Although the city walls were a security necessity in the 18th century, they were an impediment to merchants, so gates such as Porte Saint-Louis were cut into the fortifications to improve the flow of commerce.

**(7) L'Îlot des Palais**
MAP K4 ■ 8 Rue Valliére ■ Open Jan–May: 1–4:30pm Thu & Fri, 10am–5pm Sat & Sun; Jun & Oct: 10am–5pm Tue–Sun (Jul–early Sep: daily) ■ Adm

Quebec City's history is interpreted in a number of interactive displays.

**(8) Hôtel du Parlement**
MAP K5 ■ 1045 Rue des Parlementaires ■ Open Sep–Jun: 8am–5pm Mon– Fri; Jun–Sep: 8:30am–4:30pm Mon–Fri, 9:30am–4:30pm Sat & Sun

The city's political forum is housed in this imposing structure.

**(9) Maison Chevalier**
MAP M5 ■ 50 Rue de Marché Champlain ■ Open Jun–Sep: 10am–5pm daily

This former inn has displays on 17th- and 18th-century Quebec.

**(10) Musée des Ursulines de Québec**
MAP L5 ■ 12 Rue Donnaconna ■ Open 10am–5pm Tue–Sun (from 1pm Oct–Apr) ■ Adm

Housed in a 17th-century convent, exhibits tell the story of the first school for girls established here.

# Other Attractions

### 1 Musée du Fort
MAP L5 ■ 10 Rue Ste-Anne
■ Open Apr–Oct: 10am–5pm daily;
Nov, Feb–Mar: 11am–4pm Thu–Sun
■ Adm

State-of-the-art technology has created a diorama that illustrates the tale of this walled city.

### 2 Bastion du Roy Lookout
MAP L5 ■ End of Rue de la Porte

Come here for incredible views of Île d'Orléans, the St Lawrence River, the South Shore, and Mont Sainte-Anne.

### 3 Parc de l'Artillerie
MAP K4 ■ 2 Rue d'Auteuil
■ Open May–Oct: 10am–5pm daily
■ Adm

Tour 17th- and 18th-century defensive buildings, including an ammunition factory used until the 1960s.

### 4 Les Glissades de la Terrasse-Dufferin
MAP L5 ■ Open mid-Dec–mid-Mar: 10am–5pm daily (to 9pm Fri & Sat)
■ Adm

This winter attraction features three icy toboggan runs bolting participants at 45 mph (70 kmph) down a steep 820-ft (250-m) incline.

### 5 Galerie d'art Inuit Brousseau
MAP L5 ■ 35 Rue St-Louis
■ Open 9:30am–5:30pm daily ■ www.artinuit.ca

The Inuit sculptures displayed here help illustrate the lifestyles and traditions of these native Canadian peoples.

### 6 Boutique Métiers d'Art du Québec
MAP M5 ■ 29 Rue Notre-Dame ■ Open 10am–5pm daily

Craft gallery dedicated to selling only locally produced works of art including hand-blown glass objects.

### 7 Parc National de la Jacques-Cartier
MAP P2 ■ 103 Chemin du Parc-National

Located 28 miles (45 km) from downtown Quebec City, this immense park abounds with lakes, mountains, and outdoor activities in all seasons.

**Parc National de la Jacques-Cartier**

### 8 Station Touristique Duchesnay
MAP N3 ■ 140 Montée de l'Auberge, Sainte Catherine de la Jacques Cartier

To see the glorious Canadian forests, head west toward Sainte-Catherine-de-la-Jacques-Cartier. This region has a Scandinavian spa, a riot of winter attractions, and watersports on Lac Saint-Joseph.

### 9 Grand Canyon des Chutes Sainte-Anne
MAP P3 ■ Route 138 est, Beaupré ■ Adm

Only 30 minutes outside the city is a series of waterfalls contained in a narrow canyon. A breathtaking sight.

### 10 Chemin du Roy
MAP P3

The "King's Road" (route 138) winds from Montreal to Quebec. Chemin du Roy is known today by cyclists as the Route Verte for its beautiful bike path that trails alongside the St Lawrence River.

**Sculpture, Musée d'art Inuit Brousseau**

*See map on pp92–3*

# Shopping and Markets

**Strolling on Rue du Petit-Champlain**

## 1 Rue du Petit-Champlain

 A marvelous pedestrianized shopping concourse that features fashion boutiques, souvenir shops, restaurants, art galleries, theaters, and a park. Don't miss a ride on the Funiculaire.

## 2 Simons
MAP L4 ■ 20 côte de la Fabrique

Fashions for the whole family can be purchased here. Expect impeccable service from the staff.

## 3 Galeries de la Capitale
5401 Blvd des Galeries, off rte 310

One of the busiest shopping malls in the country with over 280 stores offering fashion, electronics, groceries, books, furniture, and more. A themed area for children includes a ferris wheel, roller coaster, and skating rink.

## 4 Quartier St-Roch
MAP J6

Along Rue St-Joseph and Boulevard Charest you'll find a host of interesting boutiques, cafés, and microbreweries, as well as the famous Benjo toy store.

## 5 Place de la Cité
2600 Blvd Laurier, junction of hwys 175 and 720, Sainte-Foy

Southwest of town you will find shopper's heaven where three upscale malls converge. It has the largest concentration of exclusive boutiques in Quebec, and also a produce market and restaurants.

## 6 Marché du Vieux-Port
This farmers' market is a cornucopia of the finest produce grown in the province (see p95).

## 7 J.A. Moisan
MAP J5 ■ 699 Rue St-Jean

Jean-Alfred's establishment began in 1871, making it the oldest grocery store in North America. Typical articles on sale at this charming store include fine condiments, meat, bread and pastries, and cheeses from around the world.

## 8 Les Promenades du Vieux-Québec
MAP L5 ■ 43 Rue de Buade

This tiny shopping cluster of unique boutiques also features the delightful Boutique de Noël, where you can buy unusual Christmas decorations throughout the year.

## 9 Marché Public de Sainte-Foy
920 Ave Roland-Beaudin, Sainte-Foy ■ Rte 440

This public market is a mix between an age-old farmers' market and a contemporary grocery store. Being able to meet the grower face to face offers a satisfying assurance of the freshness of your purchases.

## 10 La Carotte Joyeuse
MAP J5 ■ 690 Rue St-Jean

Specialists in organically grown produce, this little grocery store sells baked goods as well as aromatic and medicinal herbs and spices.

# Nightlife

 **Grand Théâtre de Québec**
MAP H6 ■ 269 Blvd René-Lévesque Est

The Grand Théâtre de Québec showcases the talents of l'Orchestre Symphonique de Québec, Opéra de Québec, and an international line-up of musical stars (see p52).

 **Le Pape Georges**
MAP M5 ■ 8 Rue du Cul-de-Sac

Enjoy live music (mostly jazz and blues) from Thursdays to Sundays while sampling local cheeses and cold meats acccompanied by a wide selection of wines by the glass.

**③ L'Inox**
MAP J6 ■ 655 Grande Allée Est

This microbrewery in the city's Vieux-Port is a blessing for beer-lovers. The place has a clear passion for the stuff and offers a wide selection of homemade blondes, whites, ambers, reds, and browns.

**④ Dagobert**
MAP J6 ■ 600 Grande Allée Est

A large, popular three-storied club with live bands on the first floor, DJs upstairs, and regular theme nights and events. The action does not begin until after midnight.

**⑤ La Korrigane**
MAP J4 ■ 380 Rue Dorchester

Set in the St-Roch district, this friendly brewpub features a pretty terrace where locals can be seen sipping excellent craft beers. Enjoy the vibrant atmosphere and snack on organic meat and veggie burgers, prepared mainly from locally-sourced, seasonal produce.

**⑥ L'Air du Temps**
MAP J6 ■ 441 Rue du Parvis

A spacious and contemporary-style pub, L'Air du Temps offers more than 50 varieties of local craft beers. Enjoy live music and comedy nights with a slice of artisanal pizza or a bowl of salad.

 **Théâtre de la Bordée**
MAP H4 ■ 315 Rue St-Joseph Est ■ (418) 694 9721 ■ www.bordee. qc.ca

Founded in 1976, this attractive theater stages a range of classical and contemporary performances from poetry to Shakespeare, with sets designed by luminaries such as Robert Lepage (see p43).

**⑧ Théâtre Petit-Champlain**
MAP M5 ■ 68 Rue du Petit-Champlain

This is one of the best small theaters in North America for design, ambiance, repertoire, and location. Entertaining performances of music, comedy, dance, and modern art.

Crowds at Palais Montcalm

**⑨ Palais Montcalm**
MAP L5 ■ 995 Place d'Youville

This multi-room theater offers performances from the biggest names in music, as well as a more intimate space for emerging artists.

**⑩ Bar Ste-Angèle**
MAP L5 ■ 26 Rue Ste-Angèle

Cozy and tucked-away live jazz and cocktail bar with a vintage vibe. It also has a good selection of local beers.

*See map on pp92–3*

# Bars and Cafés

 **Les Voûtes Napoleon**
MAP J6 ■ 680 Grande Allée Est

Local live music and a snug atmosphere, plus extremely friendly staff add to the ambiance of this brick-walled subterranean bar. They also offer a selection of local beers.

 **Le Ninkasi du Faubourg**
MAP J5 ■ 811 Rue St-Jean

Named after the ancient Sumerian goddess of beer, this microbrewery also operates as a live music venue and has karaoke nights from Tuesdays to Sundays starting at 10pm.

**3** **Pub d'Orsay**
MAP L5 ■ 65 Rue de Buade

One of the city's most appealing pubs, both indoors and out, this is the perfect place to sample Quebec's famous microbrewery beers such as La Fin du Monde, Boréale, and Blanche de Chambly, and the unique taste of McKeown Cidre.

**4** **Bar Le Sacrilege**
MAP J5 ■ 447 Rue St-Jean

This quaint pub with church pew seats has 14 different micro-brews on tap, but that's not all it offers: it often doubles as a performance space for actors and musicians.

Outdoor tables at Bar Le Sacrilege

 **Cantook**
MAP J5 ■ 575 Rue St-Jean

Small but welcoming roaster and coffee shop offering a vast selection of excellent beans that you can purchase whole or enjoy on the premises.

 **Café Krieghoff**
1091 Ave Cartier ■ Bus No. 11

If you wish to venture into the heart of Quebec City's artistic community, there is no better place than a seat at this convivial café. Ideal for light meals and strong coffee, B&B accommodations are available too.

**7** **1068 Wine and Cheese Bar**
MAP L5 ■ Le Château Frontenac, 1 Rue des Carrières

Named after the year of Quebec City's founding, this stylish wine bar in the famed Le Château Frontenac pours its finest wines and offers one of the largest selections of Quebec cheeses in Canada.

 **L'Oncle Antoine**
MAP M5 ■ 29 Rue St-Pierre

One of the city's oldest surviving bars from 1754, L'Oncle Antoine is set in a stone cellar with a fireplace and an outdoor patio. Try the French onion soup with a refreshing pint of local beer.

**9** **La Barberie**
MAP J4 ■ 310 Rue St-Roch

Highlights of this eco-friendly brewery include a tasting room and a beer garden. There's no kitchen on-site but the staff will happily help you order in from restaurants nearby.

**10** **Chez Temporel**
MAP L4 ■ 25 Rue Couillard

On a quiet street, this popular meeting place has the best homemade crois-sants, *croque monsieurs* (baked ham and cheese sandwiches), and coffee in the province.

# Restaurants

**PRICE CATEGORIES**

For a three-course meal for one with half a bottle of wine (or equivalent meal), taxes and extra charges.

$ under $40   $$ $40–$80   $$$ over $80

**Elegant dining area at Café du Monde**

###  Café du Monde
MAP M5 ▪ 84 Rue Dalhousie ▪ (418) 692 4455 ▪ $$

In a lovely waterside location, this Paris-style bistro serves great food. Try the black pudding with apple compote.

### 2 Patente et Machin
MAP M4 ▪ 82 Rue St-Joseph Ouest ▪ (581) 981 3999 ▪ $$

Casual, lively French eatery with the latest fresh offerings written on a blackboard. Seafood and meat dishes are prepared in creative and surprising ways.

### 3 Savini
MAP J6 ▪ 680 Grande Allée Est ▪ (418) 647 4747 ▪ $$

Savini is a stylish "resto-bar and vinotheque" that serves classic Italian dishes and an impressive list of wines by the glass. After supper it turns into a buzzing nightspot.

### 4 Paillard
MAP K5 ▪ 1097 Rue St-Jean ▪ (418) 692 1221 ▪ $

Modern gourmet bakery and café that's buzzing at brunch and lunch time. Among the huge variety of homemade delicacies, the sweet and savoury croissants are especially wonderful.

### 5 Le Champlain
MAP L5 ▪ 1 Rue des Carrières ▪ (418) 692 3861 ▪ $$$

Landmark classic French eatery that has been reinvented over the years and serves fantastic regional cuisine.

### 6 Toast!
MAP M4 ▪ 17 Rue du Sault-au-Matelot ▪ (418) 692 1334 ▪ $$$

This chic restaurant has a secret garden terrace and serves out-standing French-Canadian food.

### 7 Restaurant Légende
MAP K4 ▪ 255 Rue St-Paul ▪ (418) 614 2555 ▪ $$$

Seasonal cuisine is taken to a high art at this esteemed restaurant.

### 8 Bistro B
MAP H6 ▪ 1144 Ave Cartier ▪ (418) 614 5444 ▪ $$

Enjoy sophisticated modern cuisine, beautifully presented, at this cocktail bar and bistro.

**Snow outside Le Lapin Sauté**

### 9 Le Lapin Sauté
MAP M5 ▪ 52 Rue du Petit-Champlain ▪ (418) 692 5325 ▪ $$$

The French country fare at this charming bistro includes rabbit-centric dishes such as rabbit pie.

### 10 Le Saint-Amour
MAP K5 ▪ 48 Rue Ste-Ursule ▪ (418) 694 0667 ▪ $$$

The amazing menu at this fine-dining spot includes wild boar, Canadian sturgeon caviar, and local venison..

*See map on pp92–3* ➔

#  Excursions from Quebec City

**Parc de la Chute-Montmorency**

## ① Parc de la Chute-Montmorency

MAP P3 ■ 2490 Ave Royale, Hwy 138 east

When the first settlers crossed the Atlantic and sailed up the St Lawrence River to this virgin area, they were greeted by the sight of these powerful waterfalls, which, at 272 ft (83 m), are higher than Niagara Falls. Take the cable car up and visit Manoir Montmorency (1781), with its interpretation center, boutiques, restaurant, and terrace with a view of the action. Other vantage points are also scattered about the park (see p34).

## ② Île d'Orléans

This lovely island outside Quebec City is dotted with farms that produce many of the fruits, vegetables, and culinary specialties of the region. Designated a heritage site with over 600 preserved buildings, visiting Île d'Orléans is a memorable experience (see pp34–5).

## ③ Basilique Sainte-Anne-de-Beaupré

This huge cathedral site is always busy with religious pilgrims, following the legacy of answered prayers touted by those who have visited this beautiful shrine (see pp32–3).

## ④ Mont Sainte-Anne

MAP P3 ■ 2000 Blvd Beau-Pré, Beaupré

A sensational outdoor playground 25 miles (40 km) east of Quebec City, the mountain is popular for world-class skiing, paragliding, mountain biking, or golfing at the 18-hole Le Grand Vallon course. With over 125 miles (200 km) of hiking trails, which double in the winter as paths for snowshoeing, dogsledding, and cross-country skiing, Mont Sainte-Anne defines the four-season personality of the province.

## ⑤ Grosse Île and Irish Memorial National Historic Site

MAP P3

Commemorating the tragic events experienced by Irish immigrants who, escaping the potato famine in Ireland, were quarantined here but died during the typhoid epidemic of 1847. Take the trolley to the village where you can admire historic buildings, and visit the 1847 Catholic chapel.

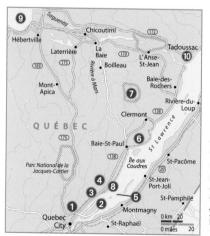

**Snow geese gather on the plains at Cap Tourmente**

### 6 Charlevoix
 MAP P2

Nowhere is the spirit and passion of Quebec Province more obvious than in this 130-mile (200-km) coastal district of rolling hills, quaint villages, and pastoral scenes. Baie St-Paul, with its heritage houses, is one of the most charming.

**Hautes-Gorges-de-la-Rivière-Malbaie**

### 7 Parc des Hautes-Gorges-de-la-Rivière-Malbaie

MAP P2 ■ Access via St-Aimé-des-Lacs on Rue Principale ■ Open daily ■ www.sepaq.com

This national park is one of Quebec's most stunning natural monuments. The steep slopes, beautiful natural surroundings, and the unusual course of the Malbaie River make this site unique. The point where the river valley takes a sharp 90-degree turn is a protected UNESCO area. Walk through the valley or, in the summer, join a guided cruise along the calm waters. You can also stay at the park overnight.

### 8 Cap Tourmente

MAP P3 ■ 570 Chemin du Cap-Tourmente

Drive 45 minutes east of Quebec City to see an incredible congregation of wild birds indigenous to the province. Over 180 species populate the area, the most photographed being the snow goose – thousands return to these fertile grounds every year.

### 9 Saguenay and Lac Saint-Jean

MAP Q1 ■ Parc national du Saguenay: 91 Notre-Dame, Rivière-Éternité

This fjord, leading inland to Lac Saint-Jean, is a designated protected area because it is frequented by beluga whales, dolphins, black bear, moose, and many other varieties of wildlife. Granite walls over 985-ft (300-m) high cast a mysterious and powerful aura over the maritime environment and give rise to the numerous fables and legends associated with the movement of its ocean tides.

### 10 Tadoussac

MAP Q1 ■ Boat trips: Croisières Dufour: 1-866 856 6668

Tadoussac's waterfront is backed by magnificent rocky cliffs and towering sand dunes, but the main attraction here lies offshore. Whale-watching boat trips take visitors out to view the minke, grey, and beluga whales in the Saguenay-St Lawrence Marine Park.

# Streetsmart

Hiker, Lac Saint-Jean,
Saguenay National Park

# Getting To and Around Montreal and Quebec City

## Arriving by Air

Montreal's **Pierre Elliott Trudeau International Airport** is the main hub of the province, serviced by local, domestic and international flights. From the airport, buses and taxis run to the city center.

**Jean-Lesage International Airport** is about 15 minutes drive from Quebec City. Several major US airlines, Air Canada, and Air Transat, a charter company with direct flights to Paris, all operate out of here.

## Arriving by Train

Montreal's Gare Centrale is where the **Amtrak** trains arrive from the US and **VIA Rail Canada** trains pull in from other points in Canada. This is also where you connect to trains or buses for Quebec City and services for other Canadian cities.

## Arriving by Sea

Cruise ships arriving in the Port of Montreal anchor at the Iberville Terminal, in walking distance of Vieux-Montréal. Within walking distance of Quebec City's Vieux-Port, the cruise terminal welcomes floating hotels to the city.

## Arriving by Road

To reach Montreal by car use either Hwy 401 from southern Ontario, which becomes Hwy 20 at the Quebec border, and cross the Pont Galipeau bridge,

or take Hwy 40 from Ottawa, crossing the Pont Île aux Tourtres. The Cantons-de-l'Est autoroute (Hwy 10) is fed by US freeways 91 and 93, with other US East Coast travelers using Hwy 15 – both lead to Pont Champlain.

Quebec City visitors can choose either Hwy 20 or Hwy 40 from Montreal, or Hwy 138 if traveling to Quebec City from the east.

## Traveling by Bus

Montreal's bus station (**Gare d'autocars de Montréal**) is at the intersection of three Métro lines in eastern downtown. There are two major bus stations serving Quebec City: **Gare du Palais**, under the railway station in the old town, and the **Sainte-Foy Terminal.**

Montreal's bus/Métro system acts as one network (the **STM**). Buses have a similar schedule to the Métro, though some night buses run throughout the night. Montreal's efficient fleet of buses covers the entire city. The Express Bus 747 operates 24 hours and is the cheapest ride between the airport and Montreal's city center. Departures leave every 30 minutes (during rush hour every 7 minutes); travel time is around 1 hour; $10 one-way, which is valid for 24 hours of travel on all STM bus and Métro lines. **Quebec City Buses** operate throughout the city. Note that both cities also have buses that serve the

surrounding region, including **Transdev Limocar** to Cantons-de-l'Est and **Galland Buses** to Les Laurentides.

## Traveling by Métro

The best way to travel around Montreal is by Métro, which is efficient, speedy, and clean. The Métro operates Sun–Thu 5:30am–12:30am and Fri–Sat 5:30am–1am. The Métro fans out to all corners of the city; some of the major interconnecting stations are Berri-UQAM, Lionel-Groulx, Snowdon, and Jean-Talon. Quebec City has no Métro.

## Traveling by Car

Parking in the cities can be a great challenge, with little street parking, short-lived meters and overpriced parking lots. However, it is very beneficial to have your own wheels. Both cities have many car rental companies, which include Avis, Budget, and Alamo.

## Traveling by Taxi

For under $10 you can move around the downtown core of both cities, in spite of rush-hour traffic. You can hail taxis from the street, or call a reputable taxi firm: **Taxi Diamond** in Montreal are reliable. Alternatively, download the **Uber** app to your smartphone and request a taxi pick-up.

## Traveling on Foot

Both cities are supremely pedestrian-friendly. The "Underground City", Montreal's vast pedestrian network of tunnels and atriums, spans the entire city. It is great for days when the weather is less than perfect. There are also clearly marked walking trails – but note that they share space with cyclists and sometimes in-line skaters.

## Traveling by Bicycle

With over 400 miles (644 km) of paths around Montreal too, there is no shortage of surface. **Bixi** is Montreal's excellent public-bike system – the first launched in North America. At $5 a pass, it features over 6,200 self-service bikes available 24 hours across the city at 540-plus stations, from April to November. A 24-hour pass allows you to borrow bikes as often as you like during that period.

Cyclists abound on Quebec City's streets, bike paths, and in the parks.

## Traveling by Calèche

In Montreal, calèche rides (horse-drawn carriages) are available at Place d'Armes, Place Jacques-Cartier, and at the foot of Boulevard St-Laurent. In Quebec City, hail one on any of the old town streets. It's a romantic, if expensive, way to get around. Rates are the same in the two cities, roughly $85 per hour, but each driver will negotiate.

## Traveling by Boat

Since Montreal is an island city, one of the best ways to get around is on the water. Shuttle boats (navettes) are in regular use, but only in fair weather, which fluctuates according to the winter ice pack. A shuttle service (**Traverse Québec-Lévis**) is available from the South Shore community of Longueuil (generally May until mid-October.)

Both Montreal and Quebec City offer a variety of boat tours (see p110–11).

## Buying Tickets and Travel Cards

The same tickets are valid on both the Métro and buses in Montreal. A one-way fare on either Métro or bus is $3.25 (exact change needed on the bus); you can also get two trips for $6 or ten trips for $27. Tickets can also be used to transfer from Métro to bus; tickets are good for 2 hours from first use.

A good bet for visitors is the one-day pass for $10, or three consecutive days for $18.

Locals often use OPUS cards, with a reloadable smart chip. OPUS cards cost a one-time fee of $6, and you can then recharge your card at all Métro stations from fare vending machines or fare collectors.

Tickets for regional trains and buses can be purchased in person at the relevant train or bus stations. They can also be bought on the official VIA Rail Canada website or at the bus stations' websites.

# Practical Information

## Passports and Visas

To enter Canada, US citizens, like all other visitors, must have a valid passport that extends beyond the length of the trip (likewise, to enter America, all visitors require a passport). You may stay in the country for up to six months, providing your passport covers this period. US and EU citizens need no visa to enter Canada, but other nationalities should check at the Canadian Embassy or **Consulate** in their home country for up-to-date regulations.

## Customs Regulations and Immigration

You are forbidden to bring certain food products, such as fruit, into Canada from abroad and sniffer dogs may operate at airports to check your luggage. Visitors over the age of 18 may import 200 cigarettes, 50 cigars, one liter of spirits, and 1.5 liters of wine.

## Travel Safety Advice

Visitors can get up-to-date travel safety information from the **UK Foreign and Commonwealth Office**, the **US Department of State**, and the **Australian Department of Foreign Affairs and Trade**.

## Travel Insurance

Health care is expensive in North America so it is essential to take out travel insurance prior to departure to avoid paying high fees should you fall ill during your trip. Make sure the insurance covers cancellations as well as loss or theft of valuables.

## Health

Montreal and Quebec City are both well-equipped with top-notch **hospitals** as well as pharmacies. Montreal also has a wide range of community health clinics (**CLSC**), which provide neighborhood residents with a range of medical and health-related services and tests. You can also find quality dental care throughout the region.

## Personal Security

Both cities are relatively crime-free, but the same precautions should apply as for any urban setting. Should you be a victim of crime, contact the police immediately. In Montreal, the **Sun Youth Organization** provides neighborhood watch teams. **Info-Crime Montreal** is a telephone and online service for reporting crime, allowing witness anonymity. All municipal **police**, **ambulance** and **fire** stations in Quebec are connected via the 911 emergency system.

## Travelers with Specific Needs

Both cities have a variety of amenities for travelers with disabilities, including on public transportation. Montreal International Airport is also equipped to assist travelers with particular requirements. Transportation from Quebec City airport can be arranged with **Transport Accessible du Québec**. The STM, Montreal's transportation authority, offers special vans for wheelchair users. Various organizations have information for travelers with disabilities, including **Keroul** in Montreal. It is advisable to call hotels and restaurants ahead of time and ask about the specific amenities available.

## Currency and Banking

Quebecers use the Canadian dollar ($), made up of 100 cents (¢). A 5-cent piece is a nickel, a 10-cent piece is a dime, and a 25-cent piece is a quarter. The $1 coin has a loon (a type of waterfowl) on it so is known as a loonie; the $2 coin is known as a toonie. French Canadians sometimes refer to dollars as *piastres*. Paper money comes in 5-, 10-, 20-, 50-, and 100-dollar denominations.

Banks and ATMs can be found everywhere in Quebec; check that your debit card uses the Plus, Interac, or Cirrus systems. All major credit cards issued by valid financial entities are recognized, but there may be associated charges. You can also exchange currency at *bureaux de change* throughout the province.

Traveler's checks are still accepted in Quebec, but if you are traveling to isolated or rural areas, ask in advance. Otherwise, you should have no problems cashing American Express, Travelex, Visa, or other major-brand traveler's checks.

*Caisses populaire*, or people's banks, while not as numerous as banks, are more amiable and give attractive rates.

## Telephone and Internet

Most international mobile phones work across Quebec. But to minimize fees, check with your local carrier about international calls, data plans, and roaming charges. You can also purchase a prepaid sim card or rent a phone.
To use public telephones (few and far between), pick up the receiver, dial the number, and deposit a flat fee of 50¢ to begin.

Canada's international dialing code is +1 (like the US). To call the UK from Canada, dial 011 + 44 + phone number. For other country codes, check www.countrycodes.org.

Many restaurants, cafés, shops, and libraries provide free Wi-Fi, while many hotels offer it for free or at a minimal daily cost.

## Postal Services

Post offices and mailboxes are available across the province. Stamps cost from 85¢ for up to 30g within Canada, to $2.50 for up to 30g for international mail. Post office hours are generally 9am–6pm daily, and until 5pm on the weekends.

## TV, Radio, and Newspapers

Quebecers have the Canadian networks CBC, CTV, and Global in English, and V, Télé-Québec, SRC, and TVA in French. Radio stations are CBC-FM at 93.5 and 88.5 in Montreal and 106.3 in Quebec, CJAD 800 AM Talk Radio for English Montreal, and INFO 690 AM for French. CBC radio and TV are funded by the goverment.

Local papers include *The Montreal Gazette* (daily) and Quebec City's weekly *Chronicle-Telegraph* in English. French papers include *Le Devoir*, *La Presse* (online only), *Le Journal de Montréal*, *Le Soleil*, *Le Journal de Québec*, and free dailies *24 Heures* and *Metro*.

Each year Tourisme Montréal publishes the official Tourist Guide, available at many outlets. Several independent cultural magazines, such as the free monthly *Voir* (French), provide readers with a guide to upcoming events and can be found in stores and restaurants.

## DIRECTORY

### PASSPORTS AND VISAS

**UK Consulate**
**MAP H1**
■ 2000 Ave McGill College
( (514) 866 5863
ⓦ gov.uk

**US Consulate**
**MAP J2**
■ 1155 Rue St-Alexandre
( (514) 398 9695
ⓦ ca.usembassy.gov

### TRAVEL SAFETY ADVICE

**Department of Foreign Affairs and Trade**
ⓦ dfat.gov.au
ⓦ smartraveller.gov.au

**Foreign and Commonwealth Office**
ⓦ gov.uk/foreign-travel-advice

**US Department of State**
ⓦ travel.state.gov

### HEALTH

**Centre Hospitalier Universitaire de Québec**
775 Saint-Viateur, Charlesbourg
( (418) 525 4444
ⓦ chudequebec.ca

**CLSC (Community Health Clinics)**
CLSC des Faubourgs
**MAP M1** ■ 1705 Rue de la Visitation, Montreal
( (514) 527 2361
ⓦ santemontreal.qc.ca

**Montreal General Hospital**
**MAP B3**
■ 1650 Ave Cedar
( (514) 934 1934
ⓦ muhc.ca

### PERSONAL SECURITY

**Emergencies**
( 911

**Info-Crime Montreal**
( (514) 393 1133
ⓦ infocrimemontreal.ca

**Montreal Fire Department**
( (514) 872 3800 (non-emergency)

**Montreal Police Department**
( (514) 280 2222 (non-emergency)

**Sun Youth Organization**
**MAP D2** ■ 4251 Rue St-Urbain
( (514) 842 6822
ⓦ sunyouthorg.com

### TRAVELERS WITH SPECIFIC NEEDS

**Keroul (Montreal)**
4545 Ave Pierre-de Coubertin
( (514) 252 3104
ⓦ keroul.qc.ca

**Transport Accessible du Québec**
( (418) 641 8294
ⓦ taq.qc.ca

## Opening Hours

Shops in Quebec are generally open 8am–9pm on weekdays, and until 5pm on weekends. However, Montreal (and, to a certain extent, Quebec City) also has numerous 24-hour options, including grocery stores, supermarkets, and pharmacies. Banks and post offices generally open daily 9am–6pm, and until 5pm on weekends.

## Time Difference

Quebec is 5 hours behind Greenwich Mean Time (GMT) – the same time zone as New York City. At midday in Montreal, it will be 5pm in London, 9am in Los Angeles, and 3am in Sydney.

## Electrical Appliances

The whole of North America operates on a 110-volt, 60-cycle electrical system, with two- or three-pronged plugs. Equipment manufactured in other countries will need an adaptor.

## When to Go

Early summer and fall are the best times to visit Quebec, when the climate is more temperate. But if you are interested in the variety of winter sports on offer, plan your visit October to November or January to March.

Christmas is magical in both cities, but it is an extremely popular time to visit. June and July are the main months for the region's festivals, so these months are also frenetic, but fun. Quebec City draws the crowds to its Carnaval each February.

The term "weather extremes" might have been invented in Quebec, where residents and visitors alike comment on variations from hour to hour. Temperatures range from 40° C (105° F) in summer to -40° C (-40° F) during winter. Packing rain gear is de rigueur and wearing layers of clothes that can be taken on and off is a sensible option.

## Tourist Offices

Quebec has a wealth of excellent and helpful tourist offices that hand out everything from maps to current event listings on request. For Montreal city, pop into the **Tourist Information Centre of Old Montreal** (open Feb–Oct), on the northwest corner of place Jacques-Cartier. **Centre Infotouriste de Montréal** also has useful information on the city and province.

In Quebec City, visit the well-stocked **Centre Infotouriste de Québec**.

The tourism office websites are equally packed with information, and are a superb source of pre-trip details, travel tips, and city news.

## Trips and Tours

Montreal and Quebec City offer a wide variety of tours. Both cities are eminently walkable, with pedestrian-friendly streets and sidewalks. Among the top walking tours in Montreal are **Héritage Montréal** and **Kaleidoscope. Tours Voir Québec** in Quebec City offers walking and food tours, as well as day excursions to the Montmorency Falls.

The Vieux-Port is the major departure point for boat trips, including the **Amphi-bus**, a bus that morphs into a boat, and the glass-topped **Bateau-Mouche**; in Quebec City, hop aboard the **Croisières AML**.

Bus tours include the **Gray Line** Hop-On Hop-Off Double Decker Tour in Montreal, and the Gray Line Quebec City and Montmorency Falls Tour in Quebec City.

## Shopping

Montreal is a premiere shopping city, with unique local fashion designers, innovative arts and crafts, and an array of culinary souvenirs, from maple syrup to ice wine. Head downtown to Rue Sherbrooke, which boasts high-end international and domestic designers, and the upscale Holt Renfrew department store. Also downtown, Rue Ste-Catherine is the city's main retail street, with mid-priced clothing and accessories stores.

Quebec City's appeal for shoppers is its antiques arts and crafts, and specialty foods, including the boutiques and galleries of the Rue St-Jean and the Quartier Petit-Champlain.

Both cities have some wonderful food markets, including the Jean-Talon market in Montreal.

## Dining

Quebec is justly famous for its cuisine, which is a robust blend of French and Québécois, as well as its international offerings.

Québécois favorites include bagels, smoked meat, and the beloved *poutine* – French fries smothered in gravy and dotted with cheese curds. Quebec also excels at cheese, with over 500 varieties available.

Quebec's wide variety of restaurants matches the diverse cuisine, from regal historic restaurants to cozy cafés to chic lounges and *casse-croûtes* (snack bars).

Throughout the Province of Quebec, *table d'hôte* menus show up at both lunch and dinner sittings. These are fixed-price deals, serving either a soup of the day or salad to start, followed by a choice of main dishes, and then a dessert and coffee or tea. It is the most economical way to dine in Quebec.

Most restaurants cater for vegetarians, and there are specialty eateries serving only vegan or vegetarian fare.

In Quebec, service personnel earn only minimum rates and depend on tips for the larger part of their wages. Although this does not excuse poor service, it is a consideration at gratuity time. Customary tipping in Quebec is between 15–20 percent of the pre-tax total of the bill.

## Accommodation

Montreal and Quebec City have a wide range of accommodations, from five-star luxury boutique hotels at over $200 a night and moderately priced B&Bs (*gîtes*), to rock-bottom hostels and university residences at under $50 a night.

In Montreal, Vieux-Montréal is one of the most popular areas to stay and is filled with a growing number of boutique hotels, many housed in historical buildings. Downtown is very central, with easy access to most parts of the city, and has everything from big-name chain hotels to smaller properties. For cozy B&Bs, try the Plateau neighborhood, while Quartier Latin, thronged by students, has a number of simple and inexpensive residences and hostels.

In Quebec City, Vieux-Québec is filled with charming historic hotels, while elsewhere in the city are larger chain hotels, lovely B&Bs and hostels and dormitories.

For a general overview on hotels, visit the Quebec Tourist Board's website.

## DIRECTORY

### TOURIST OFFICES

**Centre Infotouriste de Montréal**
**MAP H1**
■ 1255 Rue Peel
[ (514) 844 5400
w mtl.org

**Centre Infotouriste de Québec**
**MAP L5**
■ 12 Rue Ste-Anne
[ (877) 266 5687
w quebecregion.com

**Tourist Information Centre of Old Montreal**
**MAP L3** ■ 174 Rue Notre-Dame Est
w mtl.org

### TRIPS AND TOURS

**Amphi-bus**
[ (514) 849 5181
w montreal-amphibus-tour.com

**Bateau-Mouche**
[ (514) 849 9952
w bateau-mouche.ca

**Croisières AML**
[ 1-866 856 6668
w croisieresaml.com

**Gray Line**
[ (514) 398 9769
w grayline.com

**Héritage Montréal**
[ (514) 286 2662
w heritagemontreal.org

**Kaleidoscope**
[ (514) 277 6990
w tourskaleidoscope.com

**Tours Voir Québec**
[ (418) 694 2001
w toursvoirquebec.com

### ACCOMMODATION

**Booking sites**
w hotels.com
w kayak.com
w priceline.com

**Quebec Tourist Board**
w quebecregion.com

# Places to Stay

## PRICE CATEGORIES

For a standard, double room per night (with breakfast if included), taxes, and extra charges.

$ under $100    $$ $100–$200    $$$ over $200

## Luxury Hotels

### Hôtel Château Laurier, Quebec City

MAP J6 ▪ 1220 Place George-V Ouest ▪ (418) 522 8108 ▪ www.hotel chateaulaurier.com ▪ $$

This friendly hotel is in a nice spot facing Parc Georges-V and is within close proximity to the Parlement and the Parc des Champs-de-Bataille.

### Fairmont Château Frontenac, Quebec City

MAP L5 ▪ 1 Rue des Carrières ▪ (418) 692 3861 ▪ www.fairmont. com/frontenac-quebec ▪ $$$

The Château Frontenac, in the center of Vieux-Québec, astounds guests with its beauty and luxury. It's decorated as a veritable museum of Canadiana, with a birch-bark canoe and stuffed polar bear in the lobby and artifacts on its walls (see p93).

### Fairmont le Manoir Richelieu, La Malbaie

MAP Q2 ▪ 181 Rue Richelieu ▪ (418) 665 3703 ▪ www.fairmont.com/ richelieu-charlevoix ▪ $$$

This fabulous hotel, dating from 1929, features a golf course, a casino, and an idyllic setting on the St Lawrence River. The hotel attracts US presidents, Hollywood stars, and high-rolling gamblers.

### Fairmont Queen Elizabeth Hotel, Montreal

MAP H2 ▪ 900 Blvd René-Lévesque Ouest ▪ (514) 861 3511 ▪ www.fairmont. com/queen-elizabeth-montreal ▪ $$$

The royalty of Montreal hotels embodies grace and comfort. It is also well known as the location of John Lennon's famous "Bed-In" of 1969.

### Fairmont Tremblant, Mont Tremblant

MAP N5 ▪ 3045 Chemin de la Chapelle ▪ (819) 681 7000 ▪ www.fairmont. com/tremblant ▪ $$$

Golf, spas, adventure activities, boutiques, and restaurants nestled in the heart of a village setting at the foot of a mountain.

### Hôtel Bonaventure Montreal

MAP J2 ▪ 900 Rue de la Gauchetière Ouest ▪ (514) 878 2332 ▪ www.hotel bonaventure.com ▪ $$$

On top of the 17-story Place Bonaventure convention center, this hotel provides an oasis of comfort. The heated rooftop pool is surrounded by a lush garden.

### Hôtel le Crystal, Montreal

MAP H2 ▪ 1100 Rue de la Montagne ▪ (514) 861 5550 ▪ www.hotelle crystal.com ▪ $$$

The dazzling chandelier, soaring windows, and leather seating in the lobby set the tone for this chic hotel, which offers stylish rooms and suites. Guests can use the well-equipped fitness center, which has its own indoor saltwater pool. The outdoor hot tub on the 12th floor gives great views of the city.

### Hôtel InterContinental, Montreal

MAP J2 ▪ 360 Rue St-Antoine Ouest ▪ (514) 987 9900 ▪ www.montreal. intercontinental.com ▪ $$$

The InterContinental connects with the Montreal World Trade Center via an atrium, where guests and visitors are offered a bonanza of shopping and leisure options under one roof.

### Hôtel le St-James, Montreal

MAP J3 ▪ 355 Rue St-Jacques ▪ (514) 841 3111 ▪ www.hotel lest james.com ▪ $$$

This renovated 1870 building provides elegant surroundings. Conference facilities, a spa, and other thoughtful touches make one feel pampered.

### Le Germain, Montreal

MAP H2 ▪ 2050 Rue Mansfield ▪ (514) 849 2050 ▪ www.legermain hotels.com ▪ $$$

A former office building that has been beautifully transformed into a serene hotel in the midst of all the downtown activity.

It is characterized by great food and impeccable service.

## Ritz-Carlton Montreal

MAP H1 ▪ 1228 Rue Sherbrooke Ouest ▪ (514) 842 4212 ▪ www.ritz-carlton. com ▪ $$$

A landmark of old-world charm and sophistication, this elegant Neo-Classical structure attracts an elite clientele often seen relaxing with cocktails or English tea in the courtyard garden. Book well in advance.

## Historic Hotels and Manors

### Auberge Bonaparte, Montreal

MAP K3 ▪ 447 Rue St-François-Xavier ▪ (514) 844 1448 ▪ www.bonaparte. com ▪ $$

An elegant 19th-century boutique hotel in Vieux-Montréal, the Auberge Bonaparte has an excellent in-house French restaurant. Guests can enjoy complimentary breakfast on the lovely rooftop terrace.

### La Marquise de Bassano, Quebec City

MAP L5 ▪ 15 Rue des Grisons ▪ (418) 692 0316 ▪ www.marquise debassano.com ▪ $$

This stylish B&B rises over a quiet street in Old Quebec. The 19th-century decor, stained glass, and high ceilings – even the original bells used to summon the servants – mark this as an authentic legacy of Quebec's railroad history.

### Manoir Maplewood, Waterloo

MAP Q6 ▪ 26 Rue Clark, about 9 miles (14 km) north of Knowlton ▪ (450) 920 1500 ▪ www.manoir maplewood.com ▪ $$

This exquisite inn was the mansion of Senator Asa Belknap Foster in 1864, who was a Canadian railroad tycoon. The restored building features ten elegant rooms with cream-colored linens and hardwood floors, plus a wine cellar in which tastings are held.

### Auberge St-Antoine, Quebec City

MAP M4 ▪ 8 Rue St-Antoine ▪ (418) 692 2211 ▪ www.saint-antoine.com ▪ $$$

This carefully restored warehouse offers one-of-a-kind decor, a waterfront setting, and amenities such as heated floors.

### Auberge du Vieux-Port, Montreal

MAP K3 ▪ 97 Rue de la Commune ▪ (514) 876 0081 ▪ www.aubergedu vieuxport.com ▪ $$$

Soak up the atmosphere of Vieux-Montréal when staying at this beautifully restored hotel in a former warehouse on the riverfront. The lovely rooms reflect the building's history, with pine floors, wood beams, brass beds, and arched windows.

### Château Versailles, Montreal

MAP A3 ▪ 1659 Rue Sherbrooke Ouest ▪ (514) 933 3611 ▪ www.chateau versaillesmontreal.com ▪ $$$

Myth and legend circulate when speaking about Château Versailles, partly because the four townhouses that it occupies were once home to Montreal's upper crust. Today the hotel welcomes a diverse guest list of performers, artists, and writers. A complimentary breakfast is included.

### Épik, Montreal

MAP K3 ▪ 171 Rue St-Paul Ouest ▪ (514) 842 2634 ▪ www.epikmontreal.com ▪ $$$

This beautifully restored 1723 building has been transformed into a sleek boutique hotel, but the history shines through, from the hardwood floors and original stone to the beamed ceilings. Plus, you can enjoy amenities like rain showers, fireplaces, and complimentary breakfast served in a skylit nook.

### Hostellerie Pierre du Calvet 1725, Montreal

MAP L3 ▪ 405 Rue Bonsecours ▪ (514) 282 1725 ▪ www.pierre ducalvet.ca ▪ $$$

Four-poster beds, heavy window sashes, and ornate furnishings cast visitors back to the early 1700s. Beamed ceilings, family heirlooms, and rich French cuisine complete the package. Lovely breakfast atrium and lounge for cocktails.

### Le Saint-Sulpice, Montreal

MAP K3 ▪ 414 Rue St-Sulpice ▪ (514) 288 1000 ▪ www.lesaint sulpice.com ▪ $$$

Literally steps from all the main attractions, yet with an inner courtyard that creates a core of tranquility at the heart of the mayhem.

## Manoir Hovey, North Hatley

MAP Q6 ▪ 575 Chemin Hovey ▪ (819) 842 2421 ▪ www.manoirhovey.com ▪ $$$

This early 20th-century inn with white columns, palatial grounds, and antique-filled rooms, sits on the shores of Lake Massawippi. The Le Hatley restaurant has breathtaking views.

## Boutique Hotels

### ALT Hotel Griffintown, Montreal

MAP H2 ▪ 120 Rue Peel ▪ (844) 823 8120 ▪ www. althotels.com ▪ $$

This trendy hotel reflects the style of its hip neighborhood, with chic furnishings, recycled brick from the district's old buildings, and modern rooms with plump beds and cotton sheets.

### Auberge Manoir le Tricorne, North Hatley

MAP Q6 ▪ 50 Chemin Gosselin ▪ (819) 842 4522 ▪ www.manoirle tricorne.com ▪ $$

The perfect intimate location overlooking Lake Massawippi and offering 90 acres (36 ha) of land. Every effort is made to accommodate travelers' needs.

### Le Pleasant, Sutton

MAP Q6 ▪ 1 Rue Pleasant, about 16 miles (25 km) south of Knowlton ▪ (450) 538 6188 ▪ www.le pleasant.com ▪ $$

Relax at this elegant boutique B&B, with dark-wood ceilings that are offset by snow-white sofas and colorful art. Le Pleasant capitalizes on its proximity to Mont Sutton with excellent ski deals.

### Hôtel du Vieux-Quebec, Quebec City

MAP K4 ▪ 1190 Rue St-Jean ▪ (418) 800 7542 ▪ www.hvq.com ▪ $$$

Centrally located, modern hotel with a welcoming lounge area. Complimentary walking tours plus breakfast baskets which are delivered to your room each morning.

### Hôtel Gault, Montreal

MAP J3 ▪ 449 Rue Ste-Hélène ▪ (514) 904 1616 ▪ www.hotelgault.com ▪ $$$

The individually styled loft rooms, set in an 1871 warehouse, are a design-lover's dream, with Scandinavian fixtures and white-oak paneling, while the bathrooms have sleek freestanding tubs and heated floors.

### Hôtel Nelligan, Montreal

MAP K3 ▪ 106 Rue St-Paul Ouest ▪ (514) 788 2040 ▪ www.hotel nelligan.com ▪ $$$

The Nelligan embraces the concept of boutique hotels, mixing contemporary furnishings with historic elements and designer decor. Features include a roof terrace, European cuisine, and a wine cellar, plus a shuttle bus to downtown.

### Hôtel Place d'Armes, Montreal

MAP K2 ▪ 55 Rue St-Jacques ▪ (514) 842 1887 ▪ www.hotelplace darmes.com ▪ $$$

This captivating hotel represents the crowning glory of the Antonopoulos family of Quebec, who preserved much of Vieux-Montréal's heritage architecture. Throughout the hotel's refined rooms and suites, guests will experience old-world charm and comfort. Features include a roof-top terrace and spa.

### Hôtel St-Paul, Montreal

MAP J3 ▪ 355 Rue McGill ▪ (514) 380 2222 ▪ www.hotel stpaul.com ▪ $$$

The exterior of this Beaux Arts building is deceiving, for inside is minimalist comfort and savvy design. The Hambar cocktail bar is perfect for a late-night snack.

### Le Germain Hôtel, Quebec City

MAP M4 ▪ 126 Rue St-Pierre ▪ (418) 692 2224 ▪ www.legermain hotels.com ▪ $$$

A mix of heritage details and contemporary design entice both business and leisure travelers here. In a great location surrounded by attractions, this tiny gem is a real find.

### Le Petit Hôtel, Montreal

MAP K3 ▪ 168 Rue St-Paul Ouest ▪ (514) 940 0360 ▪ www.petithotel montreal.com ▪ $$$

Bright orange pops of color play against old stone at this whimsical Vieux-Montréal hotel, housed in an elegant 19th-century building. Stylish rooms come in clothing sizes – S, M, L, XL – and the lobby café serves up potent espressos and silky red wines. Bicycles are also available for guests' use.

### Loews Hôtel Vogue, Montreal

MAP H1 ▪ 1425 Rue de la Montagne ▪ (514) 285 5555 ▪ www.loews hotels.com ▪ $$$

Larger than most boutique hotels, with a fine central location from which to explore all the sights and the nightlife of the city. It is also home to one of the city's finest restaurants, Le Société Bistro.

## Mid-Range Hotels

### Hôtel Château de l'Argoat, Montreal

MAP E3 ▪ 524 Rue Sherbrooke Est ▪ (514) 842 2046 ▪ www.hotel-chateau-argoat.com ▪ $$

Pleasant, good-value hotel in a lively neighborhood with eclectic decor. The decor in the rooms is eclectic, with a mix of modern and vintage furnishings. Room charges include breakfast and parking.

### Hotel des Coutellier, Quebec City

MAP K4 ▪ 253 Rue St-Paul ▪ (418) 692 9696 ▪ www. hoteldescoutellier.com ▪ $$

Exposed brick, hardwood floors, and wonderful city views are offered from most rooms. Breakfast is delivered each morning by the amiable staff.

### Hôtel Le Dauphin Centre-Ville, Montreal

MAP J3 ▪ 1025 Rue de Bleury ▪ (514) 788 3888 ▪ www.hotelsdauphin.ca ▪ $$

Good-value hotel featuring spacious modern rooms with hardwood floors, iMac desktop computers, Keurig coffee machines, and other

such nice extras. Fresh croissants are part of the complimentary breakfast.

### Hôtel Manoir d'Auteuil, Quebec City

MAP K5 ▪ 49 Rue d'Auteuil ▪ (866) 662 6647 ▪ www. manoirdauteuil.com ▪ $$

This charming hotel, built in what used to be a private home, is located in the heart of the Old City. While the rooms and suites vary in size as well as decor, all are warm, welcoming, and equipped with modern amenities.

### Hôtel Manoir Sherbrooke, Montreal

MAP D3 ▪ 157 Rue Sherbrooke Est ▪ (514) 845 0915 ▪ www.manoir sherbrooke.ca ▪ $$

A heritage exterior gives way to luxurious accommodations inside. Proud, friendly staff offer a 24-hour reception, suites with whirlpools, and a complimentary breakfast.

### Hôtel Terrasse Dufferin, Quebec City

MAP L5 ▪ 6 Place de la Terrasse-Dufferin ▪ (418) 694 9472 ▪ www.terrasse dufferin.net ▪ $$

Spectacular views of the Château Frontenac and St Lawrence River make for a memorable stay at this atmospheric hotel. The well-appointed rooms benefit from balconies and kitchenettes.

### Hôtel Zero 1, Montreal

MAP M2 ▪ 1 Blvd René-Lévesque Est ▪ (514) 871 9696 ▪ www.zero1-mtl. com ▪ $$

This artsy urban hotel rises over the Quartier

des Spectacles, and offers stylish rooms and suites, all with kitchens, and spectacular views of the city skyline. The trendy roof terrace also provides a relaxing space from which to peruse the city below.

### Le Château de Pierre, Quebec City

MAP L5 ▪ 17 Ave Ste-Geneviève ▪ (418) 694 0429 ▪ www.chateau depierre.com ▪ $$

A million-dollar location attracts visitors to this charming hotel. Rooms are decorated in the style of the British colonial era and maintain an air of refinement. Rooms have views of the St Lawrence River or the garden.

### Le Priori, Quebec City

MAP M4 ▪ 15 Rue Sault-au-Matelot ▪ (418) 692 3992 ▪ www.hotel lepriori.com ▪ $$

This is an imaginative little hotel where down-filled duvets and slate showers complement wood-burning fireplaces and full kitchens.

### Sofitel, Montreal

MAP B3 ▪ 1155 Rue Sherbrooke Ouest ▪ (514) 285 9000 ▪ www.sofitel.com ▪ $$

With access to galleries, museums, shopping, and nightlife, the Sofitel is a welcome mid-range chain addition to the city's supply of hotel rooms. Every frill and service is available, including excellent dining on-site at Le Renoir restaurant.

*For a key to hotel price categories* see p112

## Auberges and B&Bs

### Auberge le Canard Huppé, Île d'Orléans
MAP P3 ▪ 2198 Chemin Royal, Saint-Laurent ▪ (418) 828 2292 ▪ www.canardhuppe.com ▪ $$
Islanders recommend this shoreside inn and villa whenever guests visit, partly due to the relaxed and tasteful ambiance, but also because of the gastronomic delights available.

### Auberge Les Bons Matins, Montreal
MAP C4 ▪ 1401 Rue Argyle ▪ (514) 931 9167 ▪ www.bonsmatins.com ▪ $$
Friendly service, freshly cooked gourmet breakfasts, and uniquely decorated rooms are features of this bohemian inn. Bright, original local art adorns the walls.

### Auberge la Camarine, Beaupré
MAP P3 ▪ 10947 Blvd Ste-Anne ▪ (418) 827 5703 ▪ www.camarine.com ▪ $$
Situated at the foot of Mont-Ste-Anne's ski resort and hugging the banks of the Rivière Ste-Anne, Auberge La Camarine serves ample portions of pleasure and relaxation. Some rooms have a balcony or fireplace.

### Auberge aux Deux Lions, Quebec City
25 Blvd René-Lévesque Est ▪ (418) 780 8100 ▪ www.aubergeauxdeuxlions.com ▪ $$
Close to all the major attractions, this B&B boasts affordable but charming lodgings in a 20th-century building. There are also two family suites available.

### Auberge L'Etoile sur le Lac
MAP Q6 ▪ 1200 Rue Principale Ouest, Magog ▪ (819) 843 6521 ▪ www.etoilesurlelac.ca ▪ $$
On the shores of Lac Memphrémagog, this is both inn and restaurant offering luxury accommodations and food with a Mediterranean flavor.

### Auberge des Gallant, Rigaud
MAP N6 ▪ 1171 Chemin St-Henri, Sainte-Marthe ▪ (450) 459 4241 ▪ www.aubergedesgallant.com ▪ $$
A year-round sanctuary, where deer roam the local landscape at dawn and dusk. The comfortable rooms include all modern amenities.

### Auberge le Jardin d'Antoine, Montreal
MAP L1 ▪ 2024 Rue St-Denis ▪ (514) 843 4506 ▪ www.aubergelejardindantoine.com ▪ $$
This Quartier Latin hotel is located at a prime historic location and has friendly bilingual staff, modern accommodations, and a charming breakfast salon.

### Auberge Lakeview Inn, Knowlton
MAP Q6 ▪ 50 Rue Victoria ▪ (450) 243 6183 ▪ www.aubergelakeviewinn.com ▪ $$
Set near Lac Brome, this antique-filled inn dates back to 1874. Room packages include breakfast and dinner. The inn houses a garden with a pool, where guests can lounge.

### Auberge Ripplecove, Ayer's Cliff
MAP Q6 ▪ 700 Rue Ripplecove ▪ (819) 838 4296 ▪ www.ripplecove.com ▪ $$
Holders of the coveted Five-Star status from the Quebec Tourism authorities, this auberge garners praise from all corners for its romantic rooms, spectacular setting overlooking Lake Massawippi, and Four-Diamond dining.

### Couette et Café le 253, Quebec City
MAP G4 ▪ 253 Rue de la Reine ▪ (418) 647 0590 ▪ www.le253.com ▪ $$
This is an LGBT-friendly B&B in the St-Roch district. Choose from ensuite or shared bathrooms and enjoy full gourmet breakfasts on the lovely terrace.

### Héritage Victorien B&B, Montreal
MAP L1 ▪ 305 Rue Ontario Est ▪ (514) 845 7932 ▪ www.montrealbedandbreakfast.ca ▪ $$
Housed in a restored Victorian mansion in the Quartier Latin area, this enchanting B&B is full of character. The beautiful rooms and suites feature period furniture and private bathrooms.

### L'Auberge Spa Watel, Ste-Agathe-des-Monts
MAP N5 ▪ 250 Rue St-Venant ▪ (819) 326 7016 ▪ www.hotelspawatel.com ▪ $$
A remarkable auberge with beautiful views of Lac des Sables. A range of equipment can be rented from the hotel, including fishing

boats, kayaks, canoes, sail-boats, quad bikes, and snowmobiles.

## Auberge Le Vincent, Quebec City

MAP H5 ▪ 295 St-Vallier Rue Est ▪ (418) 523 5000 ▪ www.hotelle vincent.com ▪ $$$

This charming red-brick hotel is located in the trendy Saint-Roch district. There are ten rooms with stylish, laid-back interiors. The innkeepers here are friendly, and breakfast is complimentary for guests.

## Budget Hotels and Hostels

### Auberge Alternative de Vieux-Montreal

MAP K3 ▪ 358 Rue St-Pierre ▪ (514) 282 8069 ▪ www.auberge-alternative.qc.ca ▪ No credit cards ▪ $

An independent, art-themed hostel in Vieux-Montréal with a choice of private or shared accommodations. Bicycle and camping equipment is available for rent here, too.

### Auberge de Jeunesse le P'tit Bonheur, Île d'Orléans

MAP P3 ▪ 186 côte Lafleur, St-Jean ▪ (418) 829 2588 ▪ www.leptit bonheur.com ▪ $

Enjoy dog-sledding and cross-country skiing while staying at this rustic auberge.

### Auberge de la Paix, Quebec City

MAP L4 ▪ 31 Rue Couillard ▪ (418) 694 0735 ▪ www. aubergedelapaix.com ▪ $

This hip hostel has 60 beds with between two to eight travelers to a room. Breakfast is included.

## Auberge Internationale de Québec, Quebec City

MAP K5 ▪ 19 Rue Ste-Ursule ▪ (418) 694 0755 ▪ www.auberge internationalede quebec.com ▪ $

Single, double or dorm choices are offered, with a fully equipped kitchen, games room, and yard.

## Hotel Quartier des Spectacles, Montreal

MAP D3 ▪ 9 Rue Ste-Catherine Ouest ▪ (514) 849 2922 ▪ www.hotel quartierdesspectacles. com ▪ $

With hardwood floors and exposed red brick, this four-story building offers simple but spacious modern rooms. All rooms have a kitchenette and A/C, with a choice between shared and private bathrooms.

## Le Gîte du Plateau Mont-Royal, Montreal

MAP D3 ▪ 185 Rue Sherbrooke Est ▪ (514) 284 1276 ▪ www.hostel montreal.com ▪ $

These clean and comfortable long-stay studios are located in the heart of Le Plateau, with access to Boulevard Saint-Laurent and Vieux-Montréal. The property also has an attached rooftop terrace.

## Les Résidences Universitaires UQAM, Montreal

East Lodge: MAP M2 ▪ 303 Blvd René-Lévesque Est ▪ (514) 987 6669 ▪ West Lodge: MAP K2 ▪ 100 Rue St-Urbain ▪ (514) 987 7747 ▪ www.residences-uqam.qc.ca ▪ $

Clean and basic rooms and studios (some with

kitchenettes), as well as apartments, are available at these two Quartier Latin student residences. Guests have access to the fitness center. Open mid-May to mid-August.

## Littoral, Quebec City

3710 Blvd Ste-Anne ▪ (418) 661 6901 ▪ www.littoralhotel spa.com ▪ $

Just a 10-minute drive outside of the city centre, this heritage hotel has a modern feel to it. A 24-hour café, free parking, and spa are available. Rooms come equipped with a fridge, microwave, and coffee maker. Also on offer is the hotel's 4-star condo.

## Montreal Y Hôtel & Auberge YWCA

MAP J2 ▪ 1355 Blvd René-Lévesque Ouest ▪ (514) 866 9942 ▪ www. ydesfemmesmtl.org ▪ $

This friendly, well-run, downtown YWCA has single, double, and triple rooms, which are simply furnished but also immaculate. Kitchen, laundry facilities, and Wi-Fi access are provided for guests' use.

## HI Youth Hostel, Montreal

MAP G1 ▪ 1030 Rue Mackay ▪ (514) 843 3317 ▪ www.hostelling montreal.com ▪ $$

Rates vary at this Montreal hostelling institution, which has been in operation for more than 70 years. Located in the heart of downtown it offers affordable single rooms and dorms with up to ten beds.

*For a key to hotel price categories see p112*

# General Index

# Acknowledgments

## Author
Gregory B. Gallagher is a freelance writer, editor, photographer, musician and historian based in his native Montreal. He writes travel articles for the National Geographic Society, *Smithsonian Magazine*, Virgin Airlines, The Globe and Mail's *Dreamscapes Magazine*, Royal Canadian Geographic Society, and more.

**Additional contributor**
Annelise Sorensen

**Publishing Director** Georgina Dee

**Publisher** Vivien Antwi

**Design Director** Phil Ormerod

**Editorial** Michelle Crane, Rachel Fox, Freddie Marriage, Scarlett O'Hara, Sally Schafer, Jackie Staddon

**Cover Design** Maxine Pedliham, Bess Daly

**Design** Tessa Bindloss, Marisa Renzullo

**Picture Research** Susie Peachey, Ellen Root, Lucy Sienkowska, Oran Tarjan

**Cartography** Subhashree Bharti, Tom Coulson, Martin Darlison, Suresh Kumar, James Macdonald, Casper Morris

**DTP** Jason Little, George Nimmo

**Production** Nancy-Jane Maun

**Factchecker** Taraneh Ghajar Jerven

**Proofreader** Susanne Hillen

**Indexer** Hilary Bird

**Illustrator** chrisorr.com

**First edition created by** Sargasso Media Ltd, London

**Revisions team** Hansa Babra, Aishwarya Gosain, Sumita Khatwani, Shikha Kulkarni, Alison McGill, Kanika Praharaj, Anuroop Sanwalia, Avantika Sukhia, Hollie Teague, Stuti Tiwari, Tanveer Abbas Zaidi

**Commissioned Photography** Demetrio Carrasco, Alan Keohane, Rough Guides/Tim Draper

## Picture Credits
The publisher would like to thank the following for their kind permission to reproduce their photographs:
(**Key:** a-above; b-below/bottom; c-centre; f-far; l-left; r-right; t-top)

**Alamy Stock Photo:** Rubens Abboud 20tl, 57cb; Adwo 18bc; All Canada Photos 96clb; All Canada Photos/Pierre Philippe Brunet 86cra; Tibor Bognar 11cl; Marc Bruxelle 56bl; Canada 95cra; canadabrian 37tl; Chad Case 48tl; Ian G Dagnall 12cl, 80bl; Danita Delimont/Walter Bibikow 36cl, /Cindy Miller Hopkins 4clb, 55cl, /Rob Tilley 17tl, /Jamie & Judy Wild 35crb; dbimages/Mikael 12br, 55br; Songquan Deng 34br; Design Pics Inc/Destinations/David Chapman 41tr, 88cra, / First Light/Yves Marcoux 103clb; Vlad Ghiea 85t; Hemis/Jean-Pierre Degas 48br, /Philippe Renault 7tr, 13cr, 43t, 91cra, 97cb; imageBROKER/ Christian GUY 97cra, /David Chapman 15tr;

Andre Jenny 33br; Ken Gillespie Photography 3tl, 58–9; Terrance Klassen 11bl; Lebrecht Music and Arts Photo Library 40cb; Priyanka Madia 94br; Megapress 49cl, 75cra; Nikreates 4cra; Organica 21b; Mehul Patel 16–17; RGB Ventures/Superstock/Robert Huberman 11cra; Rolf Hicker Photography 4b, 44t; WPics/ Hal Beral 17c; Tracey Whitefoot 21tr; Xinhua 54tl.

**Bridgeman Images:** AGIP 42tl.

**Cafe du Monde:** 101tl.

**Centre d'histoire de Montréal:** 64clb.

**Centre des Sciences de Montréal:** ShootStudio /Jean-Francois Lemire 50bl.

**La Champagnerie:** David Afriat 66cla.

**Corbis:** All Canada Photos/Perry Mastrovito 2tr, 38–9; AWL/Alan Copson 47br; Bettman 41clb; First Light/Philippe Henry 87clb; Hemis/Philippe Renault 101crb; Louis Hennepin 40t; Icon SMI/ Minas Panagiotakis 49tr.

**La Distillerie Montréal:** Jessika Duquette 73tr.

**Dreamstime.com:** Bonnyblue 64tr; Michel Bussieres 4cl, 46b, 79t; Mircea Costina 84cra; Danechka 61crb; Martial Genest 2tl, 8–9, 51cra; Vlad Ghiea 62t; Christian De Grandmaison 20bl; Howiewu 86bl; Wangkun Jia 10cl, 11crb, 28cl, 28br; 31br, 32clb, 32–3, 61tl, 69br, 93tl; Meunierd 10b, 12–13, 18–19, 96tr; Mikeaubry 6clb; Martine Oger 81clb; Zaslavsky Oleg 1; Peanutroaster 28–9; Denis Pepin 11br, 37br; Photal 16clb; Pictureguy66 103tr; Isabel Poulin 53br; Sandra Richardson 29crb; Louise Rivard 46tr; Scottbeard 102tl; Think Design Manage 76–7; Jannis Werner 10cla.

**Espace pour la Vie Montréal:** Jardin Botanique de Montréal/Michel Tremblay 20cr; Claude Lafond 19bc; Planetarium Rio Tinto Alcan/ Sebastien Gauthier 4t, /Jean-François Hamelin 18crb.

**Les Fêtes de la Nouvelle-France:** Simon Armstrong 57tr.

**Getty Images:** AFP/Rogerio Barbosa 14tr, 15clb; C Flanigan 99clb.

**Holder Restaurant-Bar:** 67tr.

**Le Capitole:** 53t.

**Le Cercle:** Dylan Page 100bl.

**Manoir Mauvide-Genest:** 35tl.

**Moishe's:** Stephane Cocke 83bl.

**Mont Sutton:** Isabel Nehera 90b.

**The Montréal Museum of Fine Arts:** Photo Denis Farley 11tr, 54b; Adaline Van Horne Bequest, Photo Christine Guest, Giovanni Battista Tiepolo *Apelles Painting the Portrait of Campaspe* (c.1726); Oil on canvas; 57.4 x 73.7 cm (1945.929) 24ca; Mrs. R. MacD. Paterson Bequest, Rembrandt Harmensz. van Rijn *Portrait of a Young Woman (Magdalena van Loo?* (c.1668); Oil on canvas; 56.3 x 48 cm (1949. 1006) 24cb; Gift of Lord Strathcona and Family, Photo Brian Merrett, James Tissot *October* (1877) Oil on canvas; 216 x 108.7 cm (1927.410) 24bl; Purchase; Dr. and Mrs. Max Stern Bequest, Photo Brian Merrett, Philippe de Champaigne *The Tribute Money* (c.1663–5) Oil on canvas; 138.5 x 188 cm (1999.1) 25tl.

**MTL Cuisine:** Tapas 24/Samuel Joubert 66br.

**Musée d'art contemporain de Montréal:** John Londono 70b.

**Musée de la civilisation de Québec:** Jessy Bernier 30br, 31tl; Nicola-Frank Vachon 30–31.

**Noël Eternel:** 65br.

**Parks Canada:** Mathieu Dupuis 47cl; Miguel Legault 63clb.

**Musée Pointe-à-Callière:** 23cb; Caroline Bergeron 22–3; SMQ/Studio du Ruisseau 22bl, /Michel Julien 22crb.

**Quartier Petit Champlain:** Llamaryon/Marion Desjardins 92tl.

**Redpath Museum, McGill University:** Torsten Bernhards 68cla, 70tr.

**Rex by Shutterstock:** Canadian Press 43clb; Design Pics Inc 4cla; Fotos International 42br.

**Ritz-Carlton Montréal:** Maison Boulud/Alexandre Parent 74b.

**Robert Harding Picture Library:** Tibor Bognár 93br; imageBROKER/David Chapman 45crb; Nikhilesh Haval 14bl; Yves Marcoux 98tl; Perry Mastrovito 79crb.

**Royal Bromont:** Le Cellier du Roi par Jérôme Ferrer/Rodolf Noel 89cr.

**Schwartz's Deli:** 83cra.

**SuperStock:** age fotostock/Terrance Klassen 36–7; All Canada Photos/Robert Chiasson 34–5.

**Théâtre du Nouveau Monde:** Yves Renaud 52tl.

**Théâtre du Rideau Vert:** Jean-Francois Hamelin 52crb.

**Tourisme Montréal:** 26–7, 80t; Matthias Berthet 73bl; Canadian Tourism Commission 56t, /Alice Gao 82cla; Marc Cramer 71crb; Granby Zoo 51br; La Ronde (Member of the Six Flags Family) 50t; Le Centre Eaton de Montréal/ Stéphan Poulin 72cra; Montréal Museum of Fine Arts 69tl; Musée Marguerite-Bourgeoys et Chapelle Notre-Dame-de-Bon-Secours 60cla.

**Tourisme Saguanay-Lac-Saint-Jean:** Jean Tanguay 3tr, 104–5.

**Ville Montréal:** Daniel Choiniere 51cl.

## Cover

Front and spine: **4Corners:** Susanne Kremer.

Back: **4Corners:** Susanne Kremer bc; **Alamy Stock Photo:** Dellnesco crb; **AWL Images:** Alan Copson tl; **Dreamstime.com:** Aladin66 cl, Photogolfer tr.

## Pull Out Map Cover

**4Corners:** Susanne Kremer.

All other images © Dorling Kindersley
For further information see: www.dkimages.com

*As a guide to abbreviations in visitor information blocks: **Adm** = admission charge; **D** = dinner; **L** = lunch.*

Penguin Random House

Printed and bound in China

First edition 2004

Published in Great Britain by
Dorling Kindersley Limited
80 Strand, London WC2R 0RL

Published in the United States by
DK Publishing, 345 Hudson Street,
New York, New York 10014

Copyright © 2004, 2019 Dorling
Kindersley Limited

A Penguin Random House Company

18 19 20 21 10 9 8 7 6 5 4 3 2 1

**Reprinted with revisions 2006, 2008,
2010, 2012, 2014, 2017, 2019**

A CIP catalogue record is available
from the British Library.

A catalog record for this book is available
from the Library of Congress.

ISSN 1479-344X
ISBN 978-0-2413-5594-7

MIX
Paper from
responsible sources
FSC™ C018179
www.fsc.org

# Phrase Book

## In Emergency

| | | |
|---|---|---|
| Help! | **Au secours!** | *oh sekoor* |
| Stop! | **Arrêtez!** | *aret-ay* |
| Call a doctor! | **Appelez un médecin!** | *apuh-lay uñ medsañ* |
| Call an ambulance! | **Appelez une ambulance!** | *apuh-lay oon oñboo-loñs* |
| Call the police! | **Appelez la police!** | *apuh-lay lah poh-lees* |
| Call the fire department! | **Appelez les pompiers!** | *apuh-lay leh poñ-peeyay* |

## Communication Essentials

| | | |
|---|---|---|
| Yes/No | **Oui/ Non** | *wee/noñ* |
| Please | **S'il vous plaît** | *seel voo play* |
| Thank you | **Merci** | *mer-see* |
| Excuse me | **Excusez-moi** | *exkoo-zay mwah* |
| Hello | **Bonjour** | *boñzhoor* |
| Goodbye | **Au revoir** | *oh ruh-vwar* |
| Good night | **Bonsoir** | *boñ-swar* |
| What? | **Quel, quelle?** | *kel, kel* |
| When? | **Quand?** | *koñ* |
| Why? | **Pourquoi?** | *poor-kwah* |
| Where? | **Où?** | *oo* |

## Useful Phrases

| | | |
|---|---|---|
| How are you? | **Comment allez-vous?** | *kom-moñ talay voo* |
| Very well | **Très bien** | *treh byañ* |
| Pleased to meet you. | **Enchanté de faire votre connaissance.** | *oñshoñ-tay duh fehr votr kon-ay-sans* |
| Where is/are…? | **Où est/sont…?** | *oo ay/soñ* |
| Which way to…? | **Quelle est la direction pour…?** | *kel ay lah deer-ek-syoñ poor* |
| Do you speak English? | **Parlez-vous anglais?** | *par-lay voo oñg-lay* |
| I don't understand. | **Je ne comprends pas.** | *zhuh nuh kom-proñ pah* |
| I'm sorry. | **Excusez-moi.** | *exkoo-zay mwah* |

## Useful Words

| | | |
|---|---|---|
| big | **grand** | *groñ* |
| small | **petit** | *puh-tee* |
| hot | **chaud** | *show* |
| cold | **froid** | *frwah* |
| good | **bon** | *boñ* |
| bad | **mauvais** | *moh-veh* |
| open | **ouvert** | *oo-ver* |
| closed | **fermé** | *fer-meh* |
| left | **gauche** | *gohsh* |
| right | **droite** | *drwaht* |
| straight ahead | **tout droit** | *too drwah* |
| entrance | **l'entrée** | *l'on-tray* |
| exit | **la sortie** | *sor-tee* |

## Shopping

| | | |
|---|---|---|
| How much does this cost? | **C'est combien s'il vous plaît?** | *say kom-byañ seel voo play* |
| I would like… | **je voudrais…** | *zhuh voo-dray* |
| Do you have? | **Est-ce que vous avez?** | *es-kuh voo zavay* |
| What time do you open? | **A quelle heure vous êtes ouvert?** | *ah kel urr voo zet oo-ver* |
| What time do you close? | **A quelle heure vous êtes fermé?** | *ah kel urr voo zet fer-may* |
| This one. | **Celui-ci.** | *suhl-wee-see* |
| That one. | **Celui-là.** | *suhl-wee-lah* |
| expensive | **cher** | *shehr* |

| | | |
|---|---|---|
| Do you take credit cards? | **Est-ce que vous acceptez les cartes de crédit?** | *es-kuh voo zaksept-ay leh kart duh krehdee* |
| cheap | **pas cher, bon marché** | *pah shehr, boñ mar-shay* |
| size, clothes | **la taille** | *tye* |
| size, shoes | **la pointure** | *pwañ-tur* |
| white | **blanc** | *bloñ* |
| black | **noir** | *nwahr* |
| red | **rouge** | *roozh* |
| yellow | **jaune** | *zhohwn* |
| green | **vert** | *vehr* |
| blue | **bleu** | *bluh* |

## Types of Shop

| | | |
|---|---|---|
| antique store | **le magasin d'antiquités** | *maga-zañ d'oñteekee-tay* |
| bakery | **la boulangerie** | *booloñ-zhuree* |
| bank | **la banque** | *boñk* |
| bookstore | **la librairie** | *lee-brehree* |
| cake shop | **la pâtisserie** | *patee-sree* |
| cheese shop | **la fromagerie** | *fromazh-ree* |
| chemist | **la pharmacie** | *farmah-see* |
| convenience | **le dépanneur** | *deh-pan-urstore* |
| department store | **le grand magasin** | *groñ maga-zañ* |
| delicatessen | **la charcuterie** | *sharkoot-ree* |
| gift shop | **le magasin de cadeaux** | *maga-zañ duh kadoh* |
| fruit and vegetable store | **le marchand de légumes** | *mar-shoñ duh lay-goom* |
| grocery store | **l'alimentation** | *alee-moñta-syoñ* |
| market | **le marché** | *marsh-ay* |
| newsstand | **le magasin de journaux** | *maga-zañ duh zhoor-no* |
| post office | **la poste, le bureau de poste** | *pohst, booroh duh pohst* |
| supermarket | **le supermarché** | *soo pehr-marshay* |
| smoke shop | **la tabacie** | *tabah-see* |
| travel agent | **l'agence de voyages** | *l'azhoñs duh vwayazh* |

## Sightseeing

| | | |
|---|---|---|
| abbey | **l'abbaye** | *l'abay-ee* |
| art gallery | **la galerie d'art** | *galer-ree dart* |
| bus station | **la gare d'autobus** | *gahr door-to-boos* |
| cathedral | **la cathédrale** | *katay-dral* |
| church | **l'église** | *l'aygleez* |
| garden | **le jardin** | *zhar-dañ* |
| library | **la bibliothèque** | *beebleeo-tek* |
| museum | **le musée** | *moo-zay* |
| train station | **la gare** | *gahr* |
| tourist information office | **le bureau d'information** | *booroh duh infor-mah-syoñ* |
| town hall | **l'hôtel de ville** | *l'ohtel duh veel* |

## Staying in a Hotel

| | | |
|---|---|---|
| Do you have a vacant room? | **Est-ce que vous avez une chambre?** | *es-kuh voo-zavay oon shambr* |
| double room, with double bed | **la chambre pour deux personnes, avec un grand lit** | *shambr poor duh pehr-son avek un groñ lee* |
| twin room | **la chambre à deux lits** | *shambr ah duh lee* |